C000173194

The Old Town
Leigh-on-Sea

Carol Edwards

ISBN 978-0-9562201-3-4

Published by Carol Edwards 2013

Sources

Southend Library
Essex Record Office
Leigh Heritage Centre
(Archivist's Team)
Kelly's Directory
The Census
Duncan Cooper
Carole Mulroney

Acknowledgements

My gratitude to all those who came forward with photographs and family memories of life on the High Street, Old Leigh. Your contributions have helped give a wider perspective of the history of the Old Town over the past decades..

My thanks to husband Barry for his technical support and photography
Chris for helping me compile this book and designing the cover
And Marion Hough for her help and encouragement.

Contents

Old Leigh

I must go down to Old Leigh again, to Old Leigh with its azure sky.
And all I ask is the right to stroll in the place where my memories lie.
With the salt sea spray and the wind's roar and white foam waves rocking,
And the warm sun on the cobbled stones and a small boat docking.

I must go to Old Leigh again for the sound of the wind in the trees,
is a wild sound, and a rough sound that shakes the tender leaves.
And all I ask is a sun filled day and the sound of the children's cries,
Their happy laughter ringing in the air, as the seagull flies.

I must go down to Old Leigh again, with its cockle sheds, candy and beer,
and walk the length of the sandy shore until I reach the Pier.
And all I ask is a Rossi's ice cream, and a ride in the playground of fun.
Then home to sleep with a dream to keep when the day is done.

Janet Denny © 2010

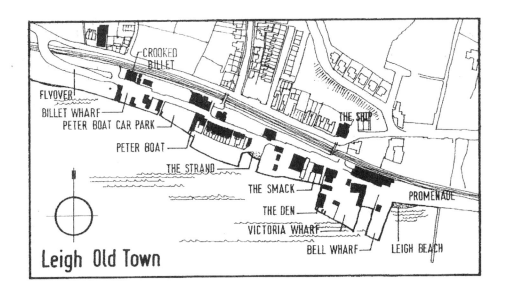

Leigh Old Town

PLAN OF LEIGH STATION, AND PROPERTY ADJOINING, IN 1876.

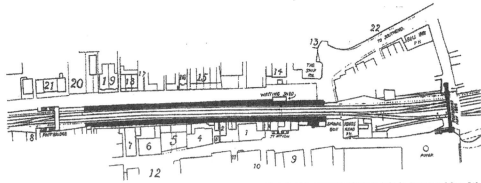

[*Reproduced by permission of Messrs. John H. Burrows and Sons, Ltd.*]

1. Mr. Busby's Grocer's Shop and Post Office.	7. Cottages.	15. Plumb's Cottages.
2. Cottage of Mr. Lungley, the old Town Crier.	8. United Brethren Public House.	16. Ray Cottages.
	9. Smack Inn.	17. Utton's Avenue.
3. Shop of Mr. F. Kirby, Ship's Chandler.	10. Mr. J. Juniper's Shop ("Constable's House").	18. Cottages.
4. Cook's Place.	11. Bundock's Yard.	19. Shops.
5. The Old Custom House.	12. The Strand.	20. Hadleigh Road.
6. Draper's Shop of Mr. H. Thompson.	13. Entrance to Eden Lodge.	21. Foster's Cottages.
	14. Eaton Cottages.	22. Site of Norman Terrace.

The Saving of Old Leigh

History plays an important part in our every day existence, yet we walk through events and past buildings, without much thought or consideration, as we deal with our own busy lives. We take for granted what has stood for centuries, often reacting to the bulldozer only when poised to demolish properties and sites of historical interest. This thankfully was not the case for the High Street at Leigh-on-Sea, Essex when the local council planned to drive a road right through the Old Town. The road to the West as it was known, was to run along the edge of Benfleet Creek, to a point east of Benfleet Railway Station where it would then have followed the line of the railway to Leigh-on-Sea. Here it had been planned to cut directly through the existing development on the High Street, severing the river frontage and then continuing on along the mud flats to join Chalkwell Esplanade. Their intention was to completely demolish the whole area to be replaced by a large promenade and this new road. Although this idea was first put forward around 1961, the council had begun buying up properties in 1949 when they purchased seventeen cottages. Three groups who were determined to save the rest of Old Leigh were The Seafront Action Group, Leigh Ratepayers and The Leigh Society. Their actions could not prevent the large flyover being built, which today brings the car into the town. The conservationists also lost the fight to ban the motor vehicle from the cobbled street, when in 1977 the Chief Constable, Sir John Nightingale said he was not prepared to support such an order. All was not disappointment as in that same year a heading in the local paper announced:

Old Leigh is Saved As Road Plan Goes West
A controversial major road plan which would have ploughed through its heart has been scrapped. The County Council's decision follows a long campaign of protest by conservation crusaders.

Some of the members of the Leigh Society celebrating their 40th Anniversary at the Heritage Centre, High Street, Old Leigh. September 2012

THE SMITHY

13A HIGH STREET
OLD TOWN LEIGH
ESSEX ENGLAND

THE LEIGH SOCIETY

HAS SAVED THIS BUILDING FROM
DEMOLITION BY CARRYING OUT
TEMPORARY REPAIRS TO MAKE IT SAFE

THE DEMOLITION HAS BEEN STOPPED
SO THAT THE SOCIETY CAN
FORMULATE A SCHEME FOR COMPLETE
REPAIR AND REHABILITATION TO BE PUT
INTO EFFECT AS SOON AS FUNDS AND
OFFERS OF MATERIALS AND LABOUR ARE
AVAILABLE; THESE WILL SUBSTANTIALLY
REDUCE THE ESTIMATED COST OF £17,500
NEEDED TO OPEN THIS BUILDING AS

THE LEIGH HERITAGE CENTRE & MUSEUM

The Leigh Society

The Leigh Society (formed in 1973) wanted to have a permanent reminder of the town's history by opening a museum. In 1979 they made a direct approach to the Southend Borough Council—owners of a large number of properties on the High Street—for a long lease on any suitable and available building. One of the places offered was the Old Smithy, because the tenant (council) either had to make the building safe or demolish it within eight weeks they were keen to find an interested party to take the project on. The Society considered this property to be of historic importance and the building to have the potential they were looking for. Having entered into an agreement with the Borough Council by the end of 1979 with the help of a local small builder, the Old Smithy was made safe. For this the society won first prize in the 1980 Essex County Council Amenity Scheme for Conservation Work. Thereafter they began fund raising and seeking grants to complete the work.

The earliest reference to a building on the current Heritage Centre site, was in 1761, later it was recorded in 1847 as being two timber framed cottages. Occupants William Morris and Son, another William, a Thomas Wade, as well as a Misters Gisby, Hurrell and Cross. George Churchyard, ironmonger/blacksmith owned the cottages in 1877 but sometime before 1880 the cottages were converted to a "Smithy". Later George's widow Mary, sold the Smithy and other dwellings in the vicinity, in 1917, to the Bundock Brothers who were boat builders. Over thirty years later Southend Borough Council brought these self same buildings and later granted a licence to the Leigh Society. It had been a long hard fought battle for everyone wanting to save this historic fishing village for future generations. The full story of this campaign deserves a book of its own. Needless to say had residents of Leigh not fought to preserve the Old Town, we would not be enjoying today what remains of the original High Street.

Leigh Urban District Council
1897-1913

The Urban District Council for Leigh was formed on the 1st April 1897, electing Frederick W. Senior as Chairman, with J. Meacham as Vice Chairman. Until the new council offices were built, the first meetings were held at the Board School on a Thursday evening at 8pm. When they moved into their new premises, the council adopted as their motif—a ship and cockleshell—which was included in a stained glass window in their new offices. One of their decisions, having seen the success of Southend in attracting visitors, was to make Leigh an inviting resort, in the hope of encouraging some of the area's visitors to get off the train at Leigh. Part of their policy was to provide a sandy beach and a footbridge over the level crossing to enable pedestrians to cross when the gate was shut. In 1897 they spent the sum of £185 to

purchase Bell Wharf, for public use and in 1899 acquired land on Two Tree Island for all important sewage works.

The Council also re-named Leigh Street to the one we are all familiar with today, High Street and lit the town by gas from the works belonging to Mr S White. In 1900 six acres of land were purchased along the seafront, so that shelters and seats might be provided for the tourist. Development of Leigh continued and in 1909 Mr Hope–Moncrieff described the area as "here now spreads a colony of smart new houses and shops, flowering out from the root of the old fishing village"

Water Supply

On the south side of the High Street near the Peter Boat Public House is the "conduit". This used to supply water to the Old Town from the 1600s that came from the spring at the head of the cliff—known as the Tikle—Tile Kiln Meadow. There were at one time two other wells in the old town. The first was in the middle of The Strand, complete with pump, later another second well was sunk near to the east of the wharf. Both wells were due to one benefactor Lady Olivia Sparrow, The Lady of the Manor.

The building is still on the
High Street today (2013)

Miscellany

Medical Officer of Health

William Douglas Watson, MRCS Eng. LRCP London, was a physician, surgeon and Medical Officer of Health for Leigh Urban District Council from 1900. As well as the public vaccinator for the Rochford and Leigh areas. He also served the Salvation Army Colony at Hadleigh, as their surgeon.

Doctor Watson was born in Tottenham, London in 1871 and was the son of a medical practitioner. He married Gertrude Florence Clarke, in 1904 who was the daughter of a retired Captain of HM Bengal Army Indian Staff. William's wife was some twenty years his junior. The couple and their children lived in Oriel House, Elm Road.

The Healthiness of Leigh.
By Dr. Douglas Watson

The ancient port of Leigh, with its small population of seafaring folk, a race whose hardy representatives today bear witness to the healthiness of the place, has been for some years gradually developing into a well-known seaside resort. Of late years this development has proceeded with a rapidity which would be amazing were it not fully accounted for by the great natural advantages Leigh possesses.

The greatest of these is perhaps its position as the nearest seaside resort to London. Situated as it is at the mouth of the Thames a few miles from the German Ocean, it may be described as an east coast watering place with a southern aspect, the pure, keen air being thus somewhat tempered. The amount of sunshine recorded for the year is more than five hours per day, while that of the summer months is nearly nine. It is worthy of note also that the very large amount of light which is reflected at low tide from the sandy flats must contribute to the efficacy of the place in effecting a cure in cases of consumption and tuberculosis, which well known physicians and surgeons are sending to convalescence.
Report complied 1908

Private Act of 1899

There was an extensive sewerage scheme to cover the whole district cost 18,000.

Newspaper

Leigh Magnet & District Mail Sat 1/2d.

Roman Coins
Numerous Roman coins have been found in the area.

1908
H Company of the 6th Battalion Essex Regiment was formed.

1911
Independent Order of Oddfellows "Loyal Old City Lodge" met at the Smack Public House.
Ancient Order of Foresters "Fishermans Pride Lodge" held meetings at The Ship Public House.
The Council and Ratepayers Association erected a footbridge from their recreation ground over the LTS Railway onto the foreshore.

Robbery from a Draper's Shop
On the night of Tuesday the 15th or the morning of the 16th, a robbery of tartans, guernseys, and scarfs was committed at the shop of Mrs J Shaw, draper, of High Street, Leeigh. From the fact that a large dog was sleeping on the premises at the time it is presumed the thief was some one known to the dog. Mrs Shaw who is inclined to be lenient, has instigated no search, and the thief has not yet been head of
Chelmsford Chronicle
Friday 25 November 1881

1890 Southend Standard
Beer tenpence a gallon
Mild Ale   10d.
Blankets   1s 6d
Coloured Felt Slippers   4 3/4d
Bacon 8d per lb
Butter   10d.

Leigh Fair was held in the Town Square (now covered by railway tracks) the first Tuesday in May.

New Road

New Road is distinctly not a new road. When the railway made its incursion it ruthlessly cut through the gardens at the rear of the houses of the High Street, this then formed a new thoroughfare on the north side of the railway, which has since been lined with new houses.

Essex Standard
Friday 24th August 1849

LEIGH.—APPEARANCE OF THE CHOLERA.—Several fatal cases of cholera have occurred in the village of Leigh, in this county. The first was that of a man named Moore, 26 years of age, who on Saturday, the 11th inst., was attacked with all the symptoms attending the disease, and in the evening death terminated his sufferings; on the Monday following his sister Mary, 9 years of age, was taken with similar symptoms, and expired the same day at twelve; and on the succeeding Wednesday the father of the above parties was also attacked and died. The next day (Thursday) there were two deaths— Mr. Balls, a basket-maker, and Mrs. Morris. These deaths were followed by that of a son of Mr. Golden Thompson on the Friday, and of Miss Forde on the Sunday. Besides the efforts of the surgeons of the neighbourhood, medicines have been provided at the expense of the the Rev. Robert Eden, brandy supplied when requisite, and money furnished to enable the poor to take the necessary precautions against the further inroads of the disease.

Building Applications

1899   Owner and builder Mr Kerry made application to build two houses.

1906   Mr Theobald submitted a plan to construct four houses

1908   Permission was sought to build a workshop at the rear of number 66 by the Gasole Engineering Company.

1913   a plan to build a workshop rear of number 31. Owners Foster/Johnson.

1914   Building application for a covered yard rear of number 17 High Street owner Mr Thompson—not applied.

1915   Mr A Ray owner—to build a shed at the rear of number 17 Alley Dock.

General Information

1927/8 Leigh Social Club met at number 81 the High Street, the Secretary was Phillip Parsons.

1935   Local fisherman built a wooden church which stood for many years on the High Street.

LEIGH-ON-SEA.

Particulars and Conditions of Sale

OF THE

Freehold Property

KNOWN AS

Nos. 72 & 73 High Street,

In close proximity to the Station and Sea.

Let respectively to Mrs. B. Taylor (a tenant of several years standing) at £24 per annum, and Mr. E. H. Tyser, at £6 per annum; together producing

PER £30 : 0 : 0 ANN.,

Tenants paying Rates and Taxes.

ALSO THE TWO

Freehold Messuages

On the East side of Quilter's Yard,

The Strand, Leigh.

Let respectively to Mr. Geo. Burden and Mr. Nathaniel Kerry at 4s. per week each, thus producing

PER £20 : 16 : 0 ANN.,

Landlord paying Rates and Taxes.

WHICH WILL BE SOLD BY AUCTION BY

Messrs. TALBOT & WHITE

At the Bell Hotel, Leigh,

On SATURDAY, Sept. 25th, 1909,

At 3.30 in the Afternoon precisely.

Solicitors:
Messrs. ARTHY & FISHER,
Alexandra Street, Southend-on-Sea.

Auctioneers:
Messrs. TALBOT & WHITE,
34 Clarence Street, Southend-on-Sea (*Tel. No. 37*).
9 Hamlet Court Road, Westcliff-on-Sea (*Tel. No. 5*).

Printed by John H. Burrows and Sons. Ltd., "Standard" Printing Works, Southend-on-Sea.

Sales

1900   Emma Beadle of Pittington House conveyance for one thousand pounds for numbers 8, 9, and 10.

1925   Sale of four houses adjacent to the railway station numbers 62-65.

1943   Albert Victor Hurst to Bundock Brothers conveyance of four hundred and twenty five pounds for the purchase of number 10 the High Street.

Strand Wharf 1930s
© Gould Family

More than Just Fishermen

The history of the Old Town at Leigh-on-Sea, usually follows the lives of the fishermen and their families, who have resided on the High Street for decades. According to Henry Newman Bride in his book "Old Leigh" the earliest records date back to 1086, this publication relates the story of the fishing industry that has grown up here, and how there came to be many changes to their way of life. My book takes up the story around 1800 and does its best—but does not always succeed in avoiding the fishing issue. I will follow the history of the public houses, gas works, coast guards, coal merchants and the coming of the railway. The honour of welcoming the Chairman of the railway company, when the train finally arrived in Leigh in 1855, fell to a Mrs Brewer, whose family had a shop in the town. In return he presented her with a gold watch and chain.

A Variety of Shops

From its earliest days, the High Street could boast of having all its needs met locally. There were butchers, green grocers, bakers, grocers, drapers, boot makers, coal merchants, and even a post office. As the train brought more visitors there sprang up cafes and restaurants, ice cream parlours.

I have researched into the lives of some of those born at Leigh-on-Sea and many others who came from around the country, looking for a new life in an old fishing village.

The High Street Underwater

Over many decades the High Street was often flooded causing damage to homes and businesses.

Flood Report

In February 1953 council minutes recorded a reported submitted by the Chief Constable and the Chief Fire Officer with connection to the flooding of Southend and Leigh-on-Sea 31st January 1953.

> *Late on Saturday night information received that abnormally high tides were expected, the Chief Constable stated that immediate steps were taken to warn the inhabitants of Southend and the Old Town Leigh-on-Sea. At 11.37 the automatic flood warning signal on the pier, sounded in central police station and further warnings were given out in the borough.*

17th February 1953

> *The transport manager reported that in order to facilitate the work of repairing the embankment adjoining the line at Leigh-on-Sea, certain lifting equipment, including lanterns, poles and wiring had been requested by British Rail.*

This view was taken in 1920. In the foreground is the small footbridge over the railway line that would have taken you to Leigh Hill

The High Street was often flooded as these pictures show

Referring to damage caused by recent floods, the pier and foreshore manager reported that eleven thousand nine hundred and forty five pounds was estimated to be the cost of carrying out essential repairs or equipment replacement.

Thirteen thousand, five hundred and seventy pounds would be required to restore properties with a further one thousand, five hundred pounds needed to complete the restoration.

Proposals for constructing mobile kiosks to replace number 5 and 9 on the High Street, as they were damaged beyond repair. Estimated cost five hundred pounds.

A Diverse and Busy High Street

As much as I would have liked to be able to show you the reader, where over the years individual cottages and shops have stood, this has proved impossible. Building names changed over the years, the census in the early days not giving numbers to the various dwellings and with the huge number of cottages and tenements demolished from the 1940's the High Street has had a an ever changing face.

Individuals and their families both transient and long term, came to fill the various dwellings, their occupations diverse and with the passing years you would see great changes in how they made a living. With education being made more readily available to poorer children, teachers employed by the local schools, would reside on the High Street. The first school was on Leigh Hill, later a more suitable building where the children could be taught was built on Church Hill. In the 1900s, Albert Moyes assistant schoolmaster, from London was Boarding with Charles Coxell, himself a schoolmaster and door or two away was Fanny Dixey also a teacher.

Albert Moyes, was born in London in 1879, came to Leigh as a teacher in the 1900s. Frederick Vernon was the local surgeon.
Photograph courtesy David Hope

During the same period Frank Bray was living and working here as a milkman. Thomas Botten from Kent had a grocers shop (which he later gave up to be a tram conductor in London!) there were also those who worked as painters/ decorators, labourers employed on the farms or at the local pottery works. With the coming of gas and piped water into the cottages, new occupations such as gas fitters and plumbers were on offer. One surprise was to find in 1860, that Frederick Emery was working as a butler! I doubt he carried out his duties in any of the local establishments.

Properties Sold Or Inherited

67 the High Street. The first reference to this house was in the will of Frances Ellen Cole in 1888. Daughter of William Rust Ritchie, who came into ownership through his mother Elizabeth, who held the rights under the will of her father William Rust. The property when on sale in 1908 was described as having a frontage of 17ft 6inches and was sold within 3 days to a local builder, Harold Edward Johnson who was also an undertaker. In 1949 the property was acquired by the council.

75 The High Street

Mentioned in the will of William Wilkin in 1851, the property was described as a coal yard, store house and carpenters shop. Occupant had been William Wilkin and seven others! His daughter Anne, who married John Say Surridge a local butcher , inherited his estate. In 1892 the property was passed down to three Surridge spinster sisters.

71 The High Street.

This property is shown to have connection with number 75 in 1892. Offered for sale in 1920, it was purchased by a Walter Tubbs, a carpenter and joiner, from Camberwell in London. With his family he moved to Leigh on sea around 1908. The property had over the years been much altered and re-built. In 1921 the building was taken over by Mr W.S.A Hibbert whose occupation was given as fish-fryer. The shop was still being used for this purpose in 1932, when an insurance policy detailed that the shop was for fried fish and chipped potatoes. The building was described as brick built, with some areas covered with weather boarding and roofed with tiles. When Southend Borough Council purchased the building in 1950 it was described as "property unoccupied"

77 The High Street.

April 1836 the widow of Thomas Rust put the property up for auction and it was purchased by John Partridge. The building offered a 30 foot frontage next to the street and was a timber and tiled messuage (cottage) In 1868 it appears that the building had been in the occupation of George Kirby for a number of years and subsequently was in the hands of other fishermen up to the year 1898 when the property was listed as:

> *A detached timber and tiled dwelling house with yard and outbuildings*
> *adjoining eastwardly to premises of Mr Ritchie, westwardly to*
> *cottages of George Surridge and in the rear of LTS railway.*

The tithe map of 1847 shows the property linked to the buildings to the west but projecting forward on to the street. By 1897 the building is replaced by a pair of cottages, still there today known as numbers 65/66 the High Street. During April 1908 there was an agreement for an exchange of land for the purpose of adjusting boundaries to have a straight boundary. In the same year William Gregory—a law clerk, took out a mortgage on the area said to be "all that land situate on the north side of the High Street, together with the brick built and slated engineers workshop, occupied by The Gasol Engineering Company" 1949 saw the purchase of number 77 by Southend Council.

In 1847 according to the map there were no buildings on this particular site, by 1854 there was a small square workshop. 1865 saw two rooms added to the High Street side on which was now a shop, the rooms were one above the other. At the same time four more rooms were added alongside , to the east of the property, to make a pair of semi detached shops. These premises became 15-16 the High Street.. A kitchen was added to the back of the building when the shop

Number 16 today.(2013)

was first used as a café. A window was added by the doorway of number 16 so that it could be opened outwards for the sale of seafood. Doorways were subsequently made to connect the two buildings. The man responsible for the development of this site , was George Fretton boot maker , who was living with his wife Elizabeth in quite primitive conditions on the site in 1850. Court rolls noted that he had erected a workshop on wasteland and was paying 2s 6d rent per annum (does not list to whom he paid the rent) During 1865 the workshop had been further extended to include living accommodation paid for by a loan of £100 from a Thomas Baxter, which was repaid within months at 6% interest. When George Fretton died in November 1877 his widow sold the land to Henry and Mary Theobald of Belton Hill farm for £180. The Theobald's then granted the "wasteland " to George Churchyard.

From 1886–1900 John Bray boot maker was at number 15, when he retired he moved further along the High Street to number 79 and his sons took over his old premises as well as number 16 next door. Alfred (1893-1944) followed his father's profession as a boot maker, his brother Frederick (1891–1947) opened a confectioners in number 16.

Number 16 in the 1960s was a sea moss and white weed gift shop. It was there from 1950 up until the 1970s

Early Shopkeepers

The Busby's originated from Kent, moving to Romford in the 1840s. The Brewers were from Southminster in Essex, both families seemed to have arrived around the same period on the High Street. They would be connected later by marriage. Thomas Busby (b1791) had a grocers shop whilst Benjamin Brewer (b1827) had a small butchers shop, but was also a Cooper , making caskets and barrels to store alcohol.

Grocers By Trade

The Busby's grocer's and later a Post Office began with Thomas Busby, following his death in 1856 his son William came down from Romford (where he was a cheesemonger) to Leigh , with his wife Ann Clube and their three children to take over the shop. In the following years their daughters Florence, Annie and Eliza were born at Leigh. Following the deaths of William in 1880 and Ann 1883, Annie and her brother continued managing the family grocery shop and post office. On her marriage to Edric Brewer the name over the door changed from Busby to her married name and the couple continued on the High Street for a few years more before moving up to Leigh Hill/Broadway. Florence Busby married Frederick Samuel Brewer (Edric's brother) Eliza Ellen Busby became the wife of George Churchyard.

Butchers and Groceries—The Brewer Family

The Brewer's shop which stood near the original railway station

The Brewers were primarily butchers by trade, their first house/ shop was opposite the old Kings Head public house. This building would be demolished after 1855 when the railway needed to build a signal box. Benjamin Brewer continued to trade in the old town as a butcher until his death in 1888, having served the town, for nearly 40 years.

Benjamin and wife Eliza had four sons. Herbert the youngest of the Brewer brothers, was the black sheep of the family. As a young man of 17, he first went to work as a butchers assistant in West Ham, later he would open his first shop in Southend, before moving back to Leigh and opening a butchers shop opposite his brothers in Leigh Road. In his youth Herbert knocked out the champion prize fighter at Rayleigh fair. Later in life he was arrested with a number of others by the police, having been caught in a shop placing bets on the Derby. A court appearance followed where he was fined. This conviction did not prevent him becoming the first Mace bearer for the mayor of Southend, but he resigned from the position directly after church parade! Marriage to Alice Aldridge came in 1888 and their only child Herbert John Samuel brewer (known as Jack) was born in 1889. Jack chose the stage rather than becoming a shopkeeper and went on to achieve some success in the West End . Tragically he was taken ill with pneumonia and died in 1915 at the early age of just 16. Albert, Herbert's brother, was his complete opposite, a quiet and pleasant individual. He married Lillian, the daughter of Count and Countess Lersner. He worked first as a butcher, then for a time was the landlord at the United Brethren Beer house before moving to London, where he had a restaurant at 651 Commercial Road. Edric Brewer, through his marriage to Annie Busby became a grocer, paving the way for his son Walker and grandsons Stuart and James to continue the tradition. Their last shop was at 84/86 Leigh Road, having first had a premises on the corner of Leigh Hill and the Broadway, but their business began on the High Street in the old town On the retirement of Stuart and James Brewer in 1986, the family had served the people of Leigh for over a hundred years. The last brother was Frederick Samuel, who married another of the Busby sisters, Florence. A butcher by trade, he left the High Street to take up a business in Alexander Road Southend. In 1888 he caught typhoid and died, leaving Florence with an eight year old daughter. Moving back to Leigh, his widow had a butchers shop on Leigh Hill and was known in times of distress to open a soup kitchen three days a week.

The Brewer's shop can be seen standing next to the original railway station.

Today Stuart Brewer still lives locally and has been a member of the Leigh Society for many years.

The Brewer's and Busby's were not alone trading on the High Street through the early 1800s. John Say Surridge(1809-1864) was both butcher and baker. His son William followed his profession and after his father's death was still in the Old Town in 1881 living with his 85 year old mother. John's brother Benjamin, first a baker later turned his hand to keeping cows (milk). From 1850-1862 John Gilson born in Wakering (1786-1862) was also a Baker, his son William married Jane Partridge in 1845, but was die just 2 years later. Henry Thompson born in London in 1820 came to Leigh around 1843 where he married Emma Joscelyne . At first he advertised himself as a Baker, Draper and Grocer, but soon was trading only as grocer and draper. The measure of his success came with a move to New Road away from the High Street. Henry was also an agent for Reliance and East of England Life insurance. George Fairchild (1805-1878) from Paglesham Essex was also a baker on the High Street in the 1860' and his business stood next door to the Brewers butcher shop.

Benjamin Barnard

Through the succeeding years there were many who earned their living as bakers on the High Street. One prominent gentleman was Benjamin William Barnard. His father George who came from Kelvedon in Essex moved to the High Street in 1838, where he worked as a baker. Benjamin was born here in 1840 and began working with his father at an early age, continuing to do so until George died in 1868. Records showed their bakery to have been at number 57 the High Street. In 1867 Benjamin married Emma Plumb, who although 10 years his junior, the union was not to produce any children. The census showed in 1901 that their address was number 28 the High Street and the building was called "The Red House" and Benjamin advertised himself as a "fancy bread and biscuit maker" His wife died in 1905 and by 1911 he was living as a lodger at number 2 Beach Avenue Leigh, where he remained until his death in 1913. Number 57 which had been his childhood home was taken over by yet another baker-Thomas Shaw who lived with his aunt Eliza who was a draper. He remained at this address after her demise and following his marriage he continued as a baker until the 1930s.

Boot and Shoe Makers

Boot and shoemakers, were commonly refereed to as "cobblers" this term however was more properly applied to a shoe repairman. Those who actually made footwear were known as "cordwainers"

George Fretton from Corringham in Essex , was living in Leigh from the 1840's until his death here in 1877. His living was made as shoemaker, as was Mathew Emery's for 30 years, beginning around the same period as George Frettons. Mathew lived on Belton Row for a number of years with his wife Eliza Robinson. Nathan Quilter who married Mary Turnnidge, was the son of Rachel Tomlin and Jabez Quilter. He was a boot maker at number 65 the High Street until his death in 1916. William Phillips born in Little Waltham Essex , came to Leigh Hill first in 1858 , before moving onto the High Street, where he remained as shoe and boot maker until in his death 1879.

Gradual Changes

As Leigh Hill developed thanks to the railway , there would be more shops opening on the other side of the line, this would in time cause the closure of shops on the High Street. With increased visitors to the Old Town for pleasure, confectioners, ice cream parlours, cafes and restaurants began to take their place. The transformation would take a decade or two but in the 1900s you would still have found grocers like Hamner Morgan, Sidney Chilcraft and Arthur Pollard traded alongside the tea rooms run by the likes of Edward Partridge. A Leigh man he advertised his business as a refreshment coffee house. Oliver Carey had a confectioners at no 21 with a Mrs Cotgrove nearby with a china and glass warehouse. In 1925 Phillip Parsons and wife Bessie were the owners of The Galleon Restaurant 75–77 (currently a storage area for boats) which used to stand opposite to where the Boatyard restaurant is today. Their son Phillip Frederick Parsons married Lillian Meddle in 1930. The Parsons were not the first to occupy this site, as refreshment rooms had stood there since 1908. The Galleon was run by A L Emery in the 1950s.

This is the wedding of Lillian Meddle to Philip Frederick Parsons in 1930.
The Galleon Restaurant behind belonged to Phillip's parents
© *C Cass*

Henry Trott had tea rooms during the 1930s as did Grace Gusterson, all of these establishments would have come about due to the number of visitors to the Old Town during the summer months.

This restaurant stood in an area known as Cook's Place

Commercial Enterprises

Confectioners

These shops sometimes provided tobacco as well as confectionary items. Sweets would have included humbugs, pear drops and liquorice all displayed in large glass jars, on the shelves. They would then be weighed on scales before being tipped into a paper bag for the customer.

John Deal

In the 1920s his confectioners stood at number 10 the High Street, previously he had been a fishmonger selling fresh fish from number 33.

Frederick William Bray

Frederick (1891–1947) was at number 16, from the late 1920s selling sweets through to the war years. He married Daisy Hills in 1925. The shop and living quarters above had previously been his childhood home. His father had used the premises for many years as a boot makers. The Bray's came to live in Leigh-on-Sea in the 1890s.

Today number 15/16 is the Strand Café a previous owner was Henry Ford in 1950.

General Stores

Robert Johnson (1865–1919) was both the chief fisherman and a grocer at number 81, from 1910–1915 his wife Rebecca Harrison kept cows on the nearby hills. Rebecca's parents were William Harrison and Mary Ann Partridge. William earned his living as a baker and milkman and his last address was at Hillside House on Leigh Hill. Robert was the son of Martha Tomlin and Robert "Skipper" Johnson.

Hanmer Morgan

Born in Hereford, in 1875, the son of a grocer's assistant Hanmer Morgan grocery shop was at number 6 during the early 1900s.

Charles Edward Watson 1841–1919

From 1864 until 1896 Charles Edward Watson's grocery business stood at number 72 the High Street. His wife Martha had the shop next door as a drapers. On retirement they moved to West Street, Leigh. Their family, all born in the old town, comprised of six sons and one daughter.

William and Herbert, both died as young men, Edward went into the grocery business for a few short years in the 1890s in his father's old shop, before moving to Devon with his family. His brother Percy took on his mother's drapers shop still at number 72, before moving the business to a premises on Leigh Hill, where he remained until his death in 1918. Charles and Martha's son Thomas, married Emma Rebecca Emery in 1894 and later in life became a Methodist Minister.

Greengrocers

At number 15 there used to be a greengrocers, during the years 1933–36 run by Alfred Henry Trott (he also had a tea room further along the High Street). In 1937 Ernest Smith was serving fruit and vegetables to the town followed in 1938 by Ralph Pickering.

Butchers

The Cotgrove brothers were first butchers on the High Street before moving to the other side of the railway and on to Leigh Hill, where their shop remained for many years.

1926/8	Horace Buck	Butcher	61a High Street
1928	Charles Tyler	Butcher	61a High Street

Refreshment Houses

Constantly changing owners or tenants and taking on new premises, offering beverages and food to the town's visitors, has been an essential part of the High Street's history. The following is a small example of those who had cafes and restaurants on the High Street over the decades.

Within a short distance of one another there was over time, a number of tea rooms coffee houses and cafes. Edward Partridge had a coffee house in 1901 at number 76. Number 70 offered afternoon tea, from 1911–1927, Edwin Casson b1865 in the Mile End London was the proprietor. James Cotgrove's coffee house was at number 39 in the 1920s. During 1928/29 Grace Gutterson was serving the refreshments (72) and in 1929/37 Alfred Henry Trott replaced her. A Miss Henney moved into number 72 in1937. That same year Harry Stone had a café at 79–81. Refreshments rooms 75–77 also in 1935/7 (now demolished) was run by Arthur Allmey Junior. Number 5 between 1948/57 was the Beach Café—owner a Mr Clarke. W T Russell's tea room from 1950–1953 was at number 77 (which would indicate that the original premises 75–77 had been altered).

Fish and Chips

Although we take for granted today that we will find fish and chip shops at the seaside and in the towns and cities it was not always the case. In 1860 a 13 year old Jewish boy named Joseph Malin, started frying chips in a downstairs room of his family's home in London. The Malin's were poor rug weavers and Joseph saw his venture as a way of supplementing their income. Later he would add fish to his chips, purchased from a nearby fish shop. At first he sold his food from a tray from around his neck as he walked the pavements in the city. As trade increased he opened a shop near to his home in London.

Leigh Fish and Chips

Although today there is a fish and chip shop at number 5 the High Street, the original fish and chip shop was at number 71. Between 1930–1933 George Henry Davies was serving this popular dish to the visitors and residents. In 1933 the shop passed to a Florence Lewis. Today many of us, would not consider it a good day out at the seaside if we did not have a bag of chips to enjoy as we walked along the promenade or sat down to a plate of fish and chips with bread and butter and cup of tea.

Number 5 the High Street, today 2013

General Companies

The boatyard today

Gregory Engineers   1930s–1950 no. 66.
Southend Engineering 1950s (owner Ian MacKenzie) no 59
H .Cole and Sons 1930s–Boat Builders
Seacroft and Co Ltd–Boat Builders no 8 (1950s)
Estuary Yacht Co–Boat Builders nos 17/18 (1950s)
Mike's Boatyard no 17 (1960s)
Davies& Mann Timber Merchants 1970s. Theobalds Wharf
Dolphin Marine Engineers 1970s
Sea King Boat Builders 1970s
Leigh Building Supply Co 1950s/70s

Port Masters

1937   J H. Elliott.
1940   J Stylers

China Shop

1908–1925 Beatrice Taylor's china shop was at number 72, selling plates, cups and other dishes. The wife of an army clerk her husband was an American born in Brooklyn. Edward Taylor died in 1921, his wife remained on the High Street with her shop until at least 1925

Frank Bridge 1877–1957

Born on the High Street where he lived with his family, Frank Bridge's first employment at fourteen years of age, was as Potters labourer. Later he would combine fishing with running his shop at number 6 from the early 1900s into the 1940s. The shop was a rubber boot stores and general outfitters for the fishing industry. In 1903 he married Lily Johnson. The Bridge family were connected to the Ritchie's by marriage when

Frank Bridge's shop on the corner.

Alexander Bridge married Mary Ritchie, another family long connected to the area. Their son Charles Ritchie Bridge 1862–1932 (one of Frank's brothers) lived at number 60. In the 1900s, he was married to Lizzie Thompson Emery. In 1949 Lizzie sold the property to Southend-on-Sea Borough Council.

Bridges Yard

Bridges Yard is thought to have stood near the Peter Boat

1837   1. Miss Baker   2 Mr William Nuggleton

1911   No 2 Thomas Hassell a labourer born in London.

1911   No 1 William Arthur Barker (Carman). A Carman was often someone employed by the railway for local collection and deliveries of parcels and goods, to and from the station. Their transport was horse driven until the arrival of motor driven vans.

1930   Frank Dunkley was living at Bridge's Yard.

Alfred Padget

Alfred Padgett came to Leigh in 1900, living first on North Street, his occupation then was commercial clerk. Within ten years he had moved to No 1 Station Road, where he would live with his family and set up his printing and photography business. However between 1923/26 his printing works were on the High Street at number 74 (his son Alan helped him to run his printing works). Alfred's postcards are among the best examples of the changing face of Essex and they are highly sought after by collectors.

Alan Padget 1893-1983, worked with his father in the family stationery business. His father Alfred died in 1958.

Late contact with Vivienne Hawkin, daughter of Thelma Easlea, provided me with photographs of Alan and Alfred Padgett.

Alfred and Alan Padget in their First World War uniforms
© *V Hawkin*

Thelma Easlea (the niece of Alan Padgett). Her father and grandfather were well known rose growers in Eastwood Essex.

© *V Hawkin*

Vivienne Hawkin Great Neice of Alan Padget
© *V Hawkin*

Alan Padget
© *V Hawkin*

It would be impossible to list all the residents of Old Leigh who have lived in the cottages and terraces on the High Street., here I offer a cross section of residents.

Henry Sheerling 1844–1902

Born 1844 in West Ham, Henry was a bricklayer and would have undoubtedly have found plenty of work here in Leigh. Henry Sheerling served in the First World War in the Royal Garrison Artillery—Labour Corps. 1866 saw his marriage to Selina Lungley (1859–1910) the daughter of a Leigh coal dealer. Together they had six children of whom one daughter Emily (1906-) married Leslie Warland, in the 1950s he owned up to a dozen boats, most of which were used as floating docks for the salvage of small craft with others used as workshops for boat repairs. In 1937 Leslie Warland's address on the High Street was number 37. Emily's brother Shaw (1880–1967) in 1911 lived at number 2 The Strand and was still living on the High Street in the Peter Boat cottages (now a car park) in the 1950s.

1911 Residents

No 56 James Ford–Coke Merchant. No. 63 George Surridge–farmer
No. 64 Walter Ellis–Plasterer. No. 68. William Lucking b Leigh-on-Sea
1849–Council Labourer.
No 69 Edmund Turnnidge b Leigh-on-Sea 1845–Postman

John Chilcraft

1900 John Chilcraft 1860–1942 born in Kent came to Leigh-on-Sea around 1902 with his wife Elizabeth and children. John worked as a general labourer and lived at number 29. The couple were to suffer the loss of three of their sons. William 1884–1902, Henry 1888–1914 (drowned) and Albert 1893–1919. Daughter Helena May 1896–1968 married William Joseph Bundock

Cottages and Tenements

No 62 William H Shakespeare b1893–1960 came to Leigh 1917. No 74 George Tickner b1877–1960 Mechanical Engineer.

The wedding of Helena Chilcraft to William Bundock

Albert Holbrow b1881 in Chelmsford lived at number 20 from 1922–1950. His previous address was No 2 Reginald Cottages. His son Stanley was born in Leigh-on-Sea 1907.

General Residents

Sidney John Reddings (1895–1977) hailed from Kent the son of a chalk maker. He married Florence Noakes in 1925. Son Sidney was born in 1927 and the family lived at 33a between 1927–34.

William John Elsen 1894–1975 was an Electrical fitter from London. Between 1930–40 he had a premises at the rear of number 4 the High Street. By 1957 William Elsen still living in the Old Town was at number 57.

The Strand
1911   1. Ebenezer Osborne. 2 Shaw Sheerling. 3 Elizabeth Lovelace. 4 Mrs Banks 5 Thomas Turnnidge. 6 Jane Houghton

Peterboat Cottages
Number 3   Francis Fennex Newland (1849-1915) Carpenter, originally from Devon, the family settled in Leigh around 1906. His son Stanley married Edith Bradley from nearby Southend-on-Sea and they lived in the 1930s at number 47 the High Street.

1950s
No.1. Mr Sheerling (resident since 1940s). No.2. Mrs Knight No. 3. Mrs Reed

1911.
No. 1. Abraham Turrnnidge (sewage attendant). No. 4. Archie Wilder. No. 5. Robert Sanders (musical instrument maker)   No.6. Albert Bearman (carman)

1950
No.2. S. Smith. No.3. Edward Hammond

Belton Cottages.
These cottages are long demolished they used to be at the far end of the High Street, at the bottom of Belton Hills.
1911
No. 13. John Hills. No. 14 Joseph Hills. No. 15 Joseph Pitt (crane driver) his son Henry George Pitt would in the 1930s live at No. 2 Bridges Yard, off the High Street.

These cottages, long since demolished were sub-standard and generally unfit for human habitation

Cottage Place (Belton Hills)

1911

No. 2 Henry Turnnidge. No. 3 Emma Sargeant. No. 4. John Axcell (bricklayer). No. 5. Joseph Axcell No. 6. William Carey (watchman). No. 7 Henry Threadgold (baker). No. 8 William Axcell

There were also cottages nearby in Townfield Place, which would be demolished to make way for the new flyover.

1911

No 1 John Axcell (labourer). No. 2. Mathew Noakes. No. 3. Stephen Meddle. No. 4. William Robinson. No. 5. Theodore Meddle. No. 6. William Turnnidge. No. 7. John Noakes

Francis Fennex Newland b1849–1915 came from Devon and was a carpenter his address was 3 Peter Boat Cottages (now gone)

In the heart of the Old Town and still there today in a slightly curved row of terraced cottages. These brick built buildings, replaced the original wooden dwellings that went up in flames when the Peter Boat caught fire in 1892

Reginald and Theobald Cottages today. (2013)

Reginald Cottages

1911

No 1 Ernest Turnnidge. 2 Albert Holbrow (Carman) lived at Leigh-on-Sea from 1906–1950. No. 3 John Johnson. No. 4 George Harvey. No. 5 George Payne (coffee house keeper).

Morgan Tudor lived in Reginald Cottages between 1957–74. One of his neighbours was a Roy Spashett.

Theobald Cottages

1911 James Henry Carey (waterman). Walter Bowers (gas worker). Ernest Cotgrove (fisherman).

1963 No. 3. Arthur Cotgrove. No. 4 Mrs Johnson. No. 5 Frederick Smith

1940s–1950s   Many of the old cottages and other buildings were being brought up for demolition in the late 1940s and into the 1950s bringing about great change in the area, during which many families left the High Street to move to other parts of Leigh.

A few more residents on the High Street.

No. 9 Stephen Ford. No. 11a Mrs Heighington. No. 12 Mrs Turnnidge. No. 13 Mrs Doncaster. No. 14 James Hoare. No. 19 Cyril Johnson. No. 22 Cyril Wood. No. 24 Riley Duncan. No. 34 Mrs Knight. No. 34a Dennis Thackery. No. 35 Henry Creffield. No. 36 Edward Mumford. No. 38 Alex Rae. No. 39a Thomas James. No. 45 Frederick Eagleton. No. 47 Frederick Blake. No. 48 Miss Cotgrove. No. 53 Mrs Thompson. No. 55 Mrs Hughes. No. 56 Frederick Cross. No. 58 Mrs Harvey. No. 62 Mrs Baldwin. No. 63 Frank Stone. No. 64 Mrs Hope. No. 65 Edward Smith. No. 68 William Eagleton. No. 69 Ernest Jopson. No. 70 Charles Baldwin. No. 74 Mrs Roskams

Other Professions and Occupations

Boat Builders

A. T. PARSONS & SON

BOAT BUILDERS

DINGHIES ALWAYS in STOCK
ASH OARS AND SPRUCE SCULLS
BOATS LET OUT ON HIRE

HIGH   STREET
LEIGH-ON-SEA

Arthur Thomas Parsons, son of a Southend-on-Sea mariner, moved to Leigh on sea after 1905, he was shown as living on Leighton Avenue on the 1911 census with his with Edith nee Ingram. Their son Frank Arthur William, was just 7 years old. Arthur Parsons was a boat builder and in 1924 paid Sidney Clayton £150 to buy the remainder of a 10 year lease for Strand Wharf In 1940 an application was made to the Borough Engineer with regard to space around the Strand:

The Borough Engineer laid before the committee a letter he had received From Messers A.T. Parsons and Sons, asking that accommodation might be provided for them in the neighbourhood of The Strand. This was to enable them to carry out a contract with the Admiralty for the construction of dinghies etc. The committee were reminded that of the seven premises acquired by them at the above position for demolition purposes to permit street widening improvement, five were at present vacant, the remaining two being occupied by tenants at the rental of 8/- per week. The Town Clerk submitted applications from each of the tenants for a reduction in rent. The Borough Engineer was directed to offer to the tenant of number 2 alternative Accommodation at number 36 High Street (belonging to the committee) at a Rental of 10/- per week inclusive and to inform Mr Parsons that subject to their being able to offer alternative accommodation to the tenant of number 5 arrangements could be made for them temporarily to occupy the vacant premises at The Strand upon terms being agreed between themselves and the Borough Engineer.

Arthur Parsons (1882–1964) and his family later lived on West Street Leigh-on-Sea , son Frank remained in the area until his death in 1975.

Sail Maker

As you would expect, there were a number of sail makers working in Leigh over the years but one whose name was well known and still prominent on the waterfront even after his death in 1968 was Francis Albert Turnnidge. Born in 1880 to George Turnnidge and Sarah Harvey, Francis began his working life as a sail maker when a young man. By 1928 he had a premises on Bell Wharf advertising himself as a yacht and general sail maker as well as manufacturing blinds, cart covers, marquees and tarpaulin covers. Today the building on Bell Wharf has a duel purpose as a police incident room on the ground floor, with upstairs being used by St Johns Ambulance on event days such as the Regatta and during the summer holidays.

Francis Turnnidge married Priscilla Cotgrove in 1905, the couple were childless. Priscilla died in 1938.

Prior to Francis Turnnidge, came Albert Angier from Brightlingsea, Essex, who used the same building, his adverts in trade magazines in the 1890s, gave his address as The Loft, Bell Wharf. In 1901 Albert Angier died.

The building is used today by The Pier and Foreshore Division as well as Essex Police. On event days/weekends St John's Ambulance use the top half of the building as their headquarters.

Wharfinger

A wharfinger is an ancient term for someone who is the keeper or owner of a wharf. They would have been responsible for goods delivered to the wharf where they would usually have a small office. They would also have been expected to deal with any disputes with regard to the day to day management of the wharf.

Samuel Field born Leigh 1827, was the wharfinger at Victoria Wharf for some thirty years. This wharf was used by the local Victorian Potteries (no longer exists) for bringing in the Kentish clay by Thames barges. Following his wife's death Samuel moved to West Ham in the 1890s to live with his son, where he died a few years later.

Wharf Superintendent

In the 1900s a gentleman with the magnificent name of Marmaduke Arthur Webb, was the wharf superintendant. Born in London in 1863, to the sone of a glass and china merchant. With his wife and some, Marmaduke Webb lived at Leigh-on-Sea until his death in 1936.

The Strand

The 1940s saw the loss of a number of buildings. Authority was given in view of its poor condition. To abolish number 72. During 1940 numbers 1 to 6 The Strand, following consideration of a report from the Chief Medical Officer for Health, who advised demolishing at once, these properties as they presented a source of danger to the public.

The Burder Family

Ethel Burder's marriage to William Biggs (local Undertaker) at St Clements Church 1913. The bride was the daughter of John Burder

John Burder born in Maldon 1851, came to Leigh in 1872, where he met and married Mary Ann Deal. At first the couple lived on the High Street, where John's occupation was listed as that of a labourer. As their family grew they moved along the street to Belton Cottages where their family grew to nine children. three sons and six daughters. By this time John Burder was a fisherman. Considering the era the children, who were born between 1874 and 1890, when the mortality rate for the young was high, the majority reached adulthood.

Their eldest child Bertrum George Burder (1874–1953) married Mary Thorpe in 1896 and they moved first to number one Belton Cottages. During this period Bertrum was a fisherman. By 1911 the Burder's were resident at number 2 Plumb Cottages on the High Street with six of their children. Bertrum was now employed unloading barges from the local dock. The couple who were still in Plumb Cottage in the 1930s when their son Eric (1922–1930) died having previously lost another son Bertrum (1905–1908). Two more children were born Queenie (1911–2001) and Stanley Bertrum (1920–1998) who became a foreshore inspector .

The man in the sailor uniform is Joseph Burder (1890–1944). He eventually left the town and became a Hairdresser. Sitting is Bertrum George Burder (1875–1953). Bertrum who with his family lived in Plumb Cottages which are now part of the Heritage Centre.

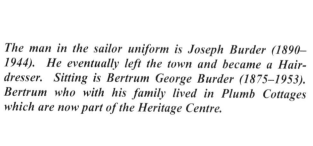

James Joseph Waller Juniper

Known as Joseph Juniper he was born in Leigh 1863 and was to become a well know fishmonger , who used to display his fish for sale on a stall outside his home. This was at number 8 the High Street. His father James, was from Gravesend in Kent, married a girl from Leigh, Selinia Waller in 1861, they returned to her home town where Joseph was born. Within a few years James and family were all back living in Gravesend where James was shown as a boarding house keeper. He had previously been a seaman. On the 1871 census they have listed as visitors John and Emma Turnidge, Emma was Selina's sister. Within a few years we find Joseph Juniper lodging with his aunt and uncle in Leigh. He would make Leigh-on-Sea his home for the rest of his life.

Joseph married Minnie Eliza Carey and had one daughter Emma who as a young woman would take up employment as a telephone operator. James Joseph Waller Juniper died in 1941.

Joseph Juniper's
fish stall

David and Kate Davies

David Gambia Ernest Davies (1870-1919) was born in London his wife Kate Dorkins came from Maldon (b1884) The couple were to meet in Westcliff-on-Sea, where David and his sister had a boarding house on Cliff Parade (previously David had been a shorthand report writer). Kate was just seventeen years old and working there as a housemaid in 1901. Twelve months later, the couple married and at some point in the next few years they moved to number 61 the High Street in Leigh. Having given up the boarding house, David Davies was now a Marine Motor Engineer, but this would be short lived as he died in 1919, leaving Kate to bring up their son David Jnr. Kate turned out to be a very resourceful and enterprising woman. One of her business ventures were coach outings.

In his will David Davies left number 61 and 61a the High Street to his wife which would be sold by his widow in 1950, to Southend Corporation for three thousand, seven hundred and fifty pounds. Described as a dwelling house, workshop and office, in what was the old United Brethren beer house. Kate Davies remained in the area where she enjoyed her retirement until she passed away in 1966.

Memories of A Leigh Childhood
Sheila Osborne

My request for information brought forth the following story of a childhood spent in and around the High Street. The provider of this wonderful historical picture of a lifestyle long gone, came from Sheila Osborne born in Leigh 1943. The following is an edited version, of her warm memories of a childhood spent in the Old Town and people she knew and met during her formative years.

Life On The High Street

To me the starting point for the High Street, begins at the beach and Bell Wharf and ends with the cockle sheds, up to Leigh Station. In the 1950s when I was a child, an annual event at Leigh was the Regatta—no resemblance to Henley whatsoever! I believe it was held late summer and located around Bell Wharf and two sections of the beach. My favourite event was the greasy pole, which was a huge telegraph pole erected vertically on the first section of beach. Attached to the top of the pole were small white paper bags full of sweets. Climbing the heavily greased pole, to release the sweets to the eager children below was of course difficult, if not impossible for some. Many attempted to reach the top but the king of the greasy pole was Jacky Marquis, who with bare chest and trousers rolled up round his ankles, would wrap his hands in rags and using chains, slung round the pole, would begin to climb. The crowd would roar and cheer him on as he struggled to the top and let the sweets fall down to the ground. Jacky and his wife Hilda lived in a row of brick cottages off Church Hill. Other

events at the regattas included, sculling (each rower has two sculls or oars) walking along a greasy bowspitt and Millers and Sweeps. This was where two opposing teams—afloat—would throw bags of soot and flour at one another!

*Cockle boats, Regatta Day
1905*

The tug of war was something we locals loved. There would be two teams one made up of Leigh fisherman the other from the police station in Elm Road. In contrast to the police officers who were neatly turned out in navy shorts and aertex short sleeved shirts, the fisherman were a motley crew of scruffily clad individuals, in tops more holes than jumper. Needless to say the fisherman always won.

Life After The War

This photograph was taken on Strand Wharf in June 1945 and was one of three victory parties in Old Leigh at the end of the war. Sheila Osborne is the little girl on the chair with her fingers in her mouth.

At the end of the war in 1945, Victory parties were held in the Old Town., I believe there were three. My family attended the one on the Strand in the June but I was just over two years of age and have no recollection of attending. 1953 saw the dreadful east coast floods and the High Street was awash with water. The residents were rowing skiffs up and down the street and I think the water line was marked on the corner of Vi's café. My Dad's Bawley was The Rainbow LO 240, along with my two brothers they made non-stop trips in her across to Canvey Island, to rescue and assist where they could. Many other locals boats did the same. My contribution as a ten year old school girl (Oak Road School, Hadleigh) was to play with the young children, who with their parents were forced to live and sleep at our school until re-housed.

On summer Sundays Bell Wharf played host to the Elim Church from Glendale Gardens where incidentally I was a "sunbeam". The Pastor in those days was George Stormont and hymns were sung accompanied by a lady called Brenda Hurrell, playing a small wooden Harmonium.

I used to visit the beach café, next door was the Thompsons shop, a little further on was the Galleon Restaurant, which I would visit on a rare occasion with my Dad. Joe Juniper's shop, as I remember was a very dark and cluttered place. On one of the High Street's corners was Natty Hoare's funny little grocers shop, which was long and narrow. She would scuttle up and down behind the counter, taking customers orders off the shelf. One day as we were going to her shop to buy my Dad's favourite sweets—liquorice allsorts Lal Ford (Henry) came out of Alley Dock and called out "don't buy the allsorts, Fat (dad's nickname) the cats been on them". Natty's cat would snooze on the rolled open sack of sweets, in the window. On the north side of the street between the Custom House and what is now Lynn Tait's Shop used to stand a row of Victorian two up two down cottages. Walter and Jane Whiffen lived in one. (Walter was from Rayleigh and worked as a refuse disposal boiler man—Jane was born in Grays, they had one son. After she was widowed and I was working in the Peter Boat part-time in the 1960s she would come in for a glass of stout. During my time at the Peter Boat ,Jack Mayo was the landlord and in the car park was a small painted hut where shellfish was sold by Ivy and Glad Osborne, my dad's cousins. The Crooked Billet (which had Osborne's as landlords for many years) had a wide path that ran alongside, leading to the level crossing—pedestrian only, across the railway track

Next to where the Coal Hole public house had stood (near the Billet) there used to be a row of four small roomed brick Victorian cottages. In 1901 my great grandparents were living at number 48—the end house. They were James and Alice (nee Lungly) Osborne with sons William and Walter, daughters Emily (known as Pem) and Maud.

"Pem" remained at number 48 converting the front room into a small tea shop. Sadly, this row of lovely cottages were demolished in the 1960s, to facilitate the construction of the hideous overpowering concrete road bridge from Belton Hills into the Old Town. More destruction and demolition was to follow.

Cockle Sheds and Osbornes

Walter Osborne and wife Annie had shed number 3, I remember Annie (born West Ham) especially because she always wore heavy decorative gold ear-rings. Number 5 shed was owned by my Great Grandfather James (Ratsey) Osborne, later the stall would be managed by his sons. My Uncle Bert's Bawley was named after his only son Norman James Osborne, who was an aircraft navigator who was tragically shot down over Tel Aviv, just before his 21st birthday in 1945. There is a memorial to him to him in the Chapel on New Road.

Locals and visitors came to the Cockle Sheds that stood along the shore opposite the railway line. The sheds are still there today serving the visitors (2013)

The Houseboats

One of my memories is of walking up a small gangway, to buy sweets from one of the houseboats moored near the station at the bottom of Belton Way. Indeed there were a number of houseboats moored along the sea wall—all gone now. The town planners and "elf and safety" have sanitised us all.

Picture taken from
The Life and Times of the Houseboats of Leigh-on-Sea,
by Carol Edwards

This photo of Sheila and her father, George
Frederick Osborne (Fat Boy) was taken in 1951.
Outside their home number 56 Fairleigh Drive,
Leigh-on-Sea.

Something to Remember

Although not just particular to the High Street I want to record something, lest it be lost! Whenever old fishermen/ Leighites met or passed one another in the street they say "Way Yer Go" with either mate or their nickname tacked on the end. I have never heard this form of greeting anywhere else and feel it must be peculiar to Old Leigh. My father always did this, never hello or good morning.

My thanks to Sheila Osborn for sharing
her childhood memories.

The Thompsons

I met Robert Nunn with his wife in 2011 when giving a talk on local history, to the Chalkwell residents association. Speaking after, Bob proudly told me of his Leigh ancestry and how his family had lived and worked on the High Street, over many decades. We arranged to meet at a later date where he talked of the Thompsons long connection with Old Leigh.

From Rayleigh to Leigh-on-Sea

Born Rayleigh Essex in 1826, John Bailey Thompson, like his father—another John—was by trade a baker. He came to Leigh not direct from his birthplace, but via Brentwood, where he had been living with his wife, daughter Ann (who died young) and first son John b1862. The family moved to Leigh where Ebenezer Henry Thompson (Robert Nunn's Great Grandfather) was born 1864. Ebenezer was always known as Pip but his family called him "Did" or "Diddy". John and wife Ann had a further seven children, three more sons and four daughters. Home for the Thompsons in the early days was number 19 Leigh Hill, before moving to a shop on the High Street. For reasons unknown, by 1891 they were back on Leigh Hill. At the grand age of 75, John, no longer a baker, was listed on the 1901 census as living on Leigh Hall Road—occupation newsagent!

The baby is Robert's mother Emily. Holding the baby is Charlotte, Pip's wife and in the white blouse is Charlotte Williams (the baby's mother)

The Next Generation

At first Ebenezer Thompson followed family tradition and worked as a baker. In 1885 in complete contrast, he enlisted as a soldier in the Army and subsequently served for two years in the South African War and was awarded "The Transvaal Orange Free State and Relief of Kimberly bars to medals". On his return home the good people of Leigh-on-Sea presented him with a magnificent clock inscribed "as a mark of esteem for services rendered to his Queen and country". Remarkably he was to serve Queen and country again during the Great War, when at 51 years of age, he joined the Navy and served on the "Seamew" government minesweeper. Eighteen months later he was invalided out of the Navy with a defective left eye.

Civilian life was perhaps not as exciting, Ebenezer worked as a bricklayers labourer and in 1889 married Charlotte Bolton whose father was the manager of the Leigh Pottery. Following their marriage the couple would have six daughters with Charlotte born in 1890 (Robert's grandmother) being their first born. In 1915 Charlotte married Frank Tyler Williams.

Another of Ebenezer's daughters Jessie married into an old Leigh family, when in 1920 she wed Theodore Meddle. Doris Bertha b1902 was Ebenezer and Ann's last child. A year after her birth, her father made application to the Justice of the Peace concerning her health. At the Essex Record office I found the following information:

> Certificate of exemption from vaccinations issued 22nd January 1903 by two Justices of the Peace, stating that Ebenezer Henry Thompson of Leigh, father of Doris Bertha, conscientiously believes that vaccination would be prejudicial to the health of the child.

Marriage entry of Charlotte Thompson and Frank Tyler Williams

Doris Bertha Thompson's ration book
First World War
Essex Record Office

Why he considered vaccination to be harmful only to Doris I cannot answer. As I was unable to find any similar objections with regard to his other children. 1911 found Ebenezer still living in the Old Town, where his occupation was shown as "unloading coal barges". Change was to take place in the following years when he turned his hand to making and selling his homemade ice cream. First he sold the ice cream from a barrow on the seafront, later he would open a shop on the High Street where he traded for over 30 years. Ever resourceful, the winter months saw him smoking roe.

Ebenezer and Charlotte Thompson celebrated their Golden Wedding in 1939. An article on the couple appeared in the local newspaper celebrating the event. Ebenezer Henry Thompson died in 1943.

Ebenezer Thompson served in the First World War, age 51.
Pictured here with his family

Robert Nunn as a baby. To his left his
mother Emily and to the right his
grandmother, behind his great
grandmother

Ebenezer Thompson in
later years

Photographs by permission of R Nunn

Ebenezer selling his homemade ice cream on The Cinder Path at Leigh.
Photographs courtesy R Nunn

Ice Cream seller unknown—in the background Bell Wharf.

Creek End Tea Garden

The idea for a Tea Room came to Dora Reynolds, in the 1980s. Born in Yorkshire in 1921, the coming of the Second World War, would see her serving in the Women's Auxiliary RAF in Nottingham, where she would meet her future husband Raymond Eric Reynolds, a leading aircraftsman RAF. The couple married in 1942. Eric (as he was known) worked as an inspector for the railway after the war, following in his father's footsteps who had been a district traffic controller L.N.E.R. Dora was to take employment when they moved to Leigh in the 1950s, first at the Peter Boat public house as a barmaid then later as a teacher at Westminster College, Westcliff-on-Sea.

Now a long time resident of the High Street (she still lives today 2013 next door to the tea rooms). The business came about, after her retirement from teaching. Dora would often find herself stopped by visitors to the old town, "they would usually ask me where they could get a cuppa on the High Street", (unlike today the pubs didn't serve such beverages). "This gave me an idea to open a tea shop in my back garden". Having applied for permission from the council to use her kitchen and garden approval of which was given in just three days allowing Dora Reynolds to launch her new business around 1980. Later the family garage would be turned into an ice cream kiosk. With her daughter Liz, they purchased second hand tables, chairs and crockery and served cream teas and ploughman lunches, to accompany the pots of tea. The café soon outgrew the back garden, but fortunately the ground next door which had been used by one of the Turnidge family and later by Snappy Noakes, became available and so her café expanded into the space. The land had previously been owned by the railway but in recent years had been purchased by the local council. Rent for the land was 2s 6d per week. When Dora finally decided to hang up her apron, daughter Liz and son-in-law Roger stepped in and managed the Creek End Café until it was sold in the 1990s.

Barmaid Peter Boat Public House

During the 1990s, Liz (Dora's daughter) with husband Roger took on the running of the Tea Rooms.

How the area looked in the 1980s

The Tea Rooms were started here in the back garden of Dora's cottage..

Dora today (2012) still living in her cottage on the High Street

Creek End Tea Garden

Southend 75647

Cream Teas a Speciality
Morning Coffee

High Street, Old Leigh

Prop.: Mrs. D. I. Reynolds

Homemade Food   *Open Daily*

A 1980s advertisement

The Tea Rooms today

Sara Williams the current owner

Ivy Eagleton

William Eagleton and Ivy Allen

During a meeting with Margaret Spurgeon in late September 2012, I was given to include in this book, information about her mother—Ivy Eagleton's Life in Leigh, taken from a brief description written down by her in 1994 .

I moved with my husband William Frederick Eagleton (b.1921) who worked on the cockle boats, nickname "Bill Brody" into number 68 the High Street in 1946. Where we lived until 1956. This was where our three daughters Sandra, Margaret and Maureen were born. Like the majority of the children in the area they attended North Street School. When we first moved to number 68 we paid rent to the sum of 14 shillings per week and this was collected by Sheila Pitt-Stanley (a well known local historian) for her grandfather the owner a Mr Meddle. Our next door neighbours were Mr and Mrs Jopson and their family. Mr Jopson was working at Leigh Railway Station during those years. Living at 64 was Walter Ellis (1880-1955) by trade a plaster. His family had lived on the High Street for many years, his father William was a platelayer and mother June a member of the Wilders, another old Leigh family. At number 70 lived the Baldwins and opposite our cottage resided Mr Noakes (Snappy) and his dog Patch—aptly named because he had one black eye. At number 21 lived my father-in-law William Eagleton (b1889) a fisherman who owned a Bawley (a boomless cutter used for fishing for shrimps and cockles). Like his father George and four of his brothers William started his working life as a labourer.

The Eagleton's lived in the middle cottage. Looking past the terrace was the old foundry now

Bernard Graham Turnidge

Beltons Row
Standing next to the white buildings is Cottage Place built in 1854. They were demolished in the 1930s.

At the beginning of this book I said I would avoid fishermen where possible, but the wealth of private unseen photographs of the Turnidge family and their friends, was not to be missed as an integral part of local history. Also their long connection with the area of the High Street now completely demolished—Cottage Place which along with other buildings stood along the bottom of Belton Hills.

I met with Bernard Graham Turnidge (known as Graham) in the kitchen of his home in Westcliff, where his passion for his birthplace in Leigh was evident. As we looked through albums of photographs, he shared memories of life in the old town where he was born in 1931 to Bernard Turnidge (1908–1995) and Margaret Tallentire (1906–1988). His mother hailed from County Durham but his father's roots in Leigh went back to the late 1700s. The couple married at The Peculiar People's chapel in Elm Road, after which they took up residence at number 11 Cottage Place (near where the flyover enters the town today). Tracing the Turnidge line back, Victoria Turnidge was mother to Bernard senior, she was born at number 9 Cottage Place in 1888. She later married a man called Stanley King. Parents to Victoria were Henry Wade Turnidge (1845–1928) and Georgiana Goshawk, who was from Suffolk. The couple lived at number 2 Cottage Place. Henry, had varied occupations—most connected to fishing—waterman/fisherman/fish hawker and labourer. Next came John Turnidge (1816–1877) wife Mary Wade. They lived on Leigh Hill. Edmund Yaxley Turnidge and Sarah Bowdell were parents to John. Edmund was born in 1789 in Leigh as was his father John (1754) and grandfather Robert (1728). By the time of Graham's birth in 1928, his ancestors had roots going back over 200 years.

My grandmother Victoria born 19th November 1887, standing next to her is her brother Edmund
© *G Turnidge*

Great Grandfather
Henry Wade Turnidge
1844-1928

Great Grandmother
Georgina Goshawk
1856-1917

Photographs © G Turnidge

My father
Bernard Turnidge
1908-1995

My mother
Margaret Talentire
1907-1988

Bernard and Margaret married in Leigh on the
2nd of June 1928
© G Turnidge

When the couple were moved from Cottage Place they lived in the last
building on the left until they too were demolished. The building to
the right is the Smack Public House which is still there today.

Growing Up in Leigh

School for Graham was North Street, where he remembered his teacher Miss Downer and the headmistress Miss Bill. After school there was the freedom to roam and play, either on the beach or the orchard, on the other side of the railway, here he recalled time spent with friends

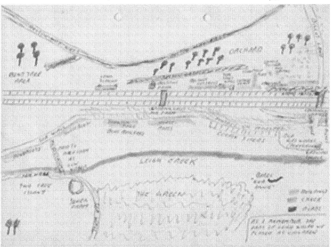

who also lived in the town—Sages, Meddles, Axcell, Cotgroves and Deals. He also talked of taking his boxing gloves to the old gas works yard (the area is now occupied by Osborne's tables and chairs behind their restaurant) and at one time he remembered there being a scrap yard on the High Street. When 17 years old he played football for Leigh Ramblers later the football team was called Leigh Panthers and Leigh Downtowners.

Graham's drawing of the area of Leigh where he played as a child

Graham Turnidge, back row third from the right.

Leigh Town Football Team in the 1890s.

Leigh Town Juniors in the 1890s.
Bundock brothers in the back row

Leigh Panthers 1950

Leigh United 1935-1936

The following list of families lived on Cottage Place (built in the 1860s) in 1937. The whole row was later purchased by Southend Council and demolished.

No 1.	Archibald Noakes	No 2	Harold Turnidge
			(great uncle to Graham)
No 3	Arthur Noake	No 4	William Axcell
No 5	Thomas Sage(basket maker)	No 6	Henry Wade Turnidge
No 7	Mary Ann Robinson	No 8	James Deal (nickname—Hungry)
No 9	Victoria King	No 10	Mrs Answorth

During 1938 number 10 caught fire and was put out by the efforts of the locals passing buckets of water along a line of volunteers. Graham would live at number 10 after 1947, having first been resident in number 11.

Nearby in Townfield Place, again demolished by the council lived these residents.

No 1	Ernest Jopson	No 2	M. Noakes
No 3	Thomas Meddle	No 4	Steven Meddle
No 5	Edward Collinge		

For Graham and others a Sunday School treat, this time in style, in Bill 'Snappy' Noakes' pleasure boat the Silver Spray. They enjoyed a visit to Walton-on-the-Naze

Marriage came in 1952 for Graham to Stella Jarvis and they lived for many years in Ray Cottages in the Old Town, with their three sons and daughter. Graham, like many earned his living as a fisherman.

© G Turnidge

Graham and Stella Turnidge today with their extended family, 2012
© G Turnidge

Graham's last comments during our meeting expressed disappointment that the cottages that had stood from the 1800s were demolished and replaced by a flyover. "They could have been restored for future generations to live in, so that they might have enjoyed what I had during my time there, living in a community rich in friendship and family".

Maureen Hume

These photographs were provided by
Maureen Hume nee Theobald.

Her Grandfather Albert Lawson used to
own a houseboat moored at
Leigh-on-Sea between the wars

VE Day 1945 Billet Wharf

Mrs Christie dressed as the Clown

My sister Benda .David with Maureen Hume standing behind him. Brother Harold with sister Dorothy in front.

A Different Perspective

Edna Hughes and her daughter Karen Ratchford, offer a different perspective on their life in old Leigh, understandably so, as one offers the memories of an adult coping with day to day to living , the other as seen though the eyes of a child.

Edna Hughes
© E Hughes

During the second World War Edna Coleman (later Hughes) served in the WAFFS – The Woman's Auxiliary Air Force Born in Bedfordshire in 1926 she came to Leigh-on-Sea with her mother in 1942, where she had rented a shop and flat on the Broadway. In 1944, whilst enjoying an evening in the Smack, Edna meet Stanley Hughes, who lived on the High Street first at number 52 with his mother (his father was away fighting the war) One evening in 1940 a knock on the door resulted in young Stanley joining the little boats of Leigh to travel to Dunkirk. Six fishing boats left that June, The Leticia, Endeavour, Resolute, Reliant. Defender and the Renown, which hit a mine and was blown up with a loss of all those on board. Their task had been to go to the shore and ferry men back to the ships moored further out.

Having reached France "Squibs" as he was known, found himself on the beach being revived by a soldier, having no idea how he got there. Later he was able to board one of fishing boats and eventually was among the lucky ones to return home. This experience did not put him off as he later joined the Royal Navy and served for six years.

Following their marriage the couple first had a room with Edna's mother but this was only temporary and in 1948 they moved to 55 High Street, where they paid rent of three shillings a week. The row of cottages were owned by the railway and had no electricity, gas or running water. Cooking was done on a range and water drawn from a tap in the town , light came from oil lamps and the outside toilet was shared with their neighbours.

Stanley Hughes
© E Hughes

Edna and Stanley had four children during their time on the High Street and washing nappies and clothes as well as keeping their home clean ,was for Edna a hard and exacting time. Although the living conditions were far from ideal the community they lived in with its village atmosphere, was friendly and supportive.

In the early 1960's their cottage was flooded with raw sewage and with the general condition of their home, which had been deteriorating for a number of years, Southend-on-Sea Borough Council declared it unfit for human habitation. They demolished the whole row of terrace houses and replaced them with a modern equivalent . Had the landlord of the properties taken the trouble and care to maintain them we would not have lost more of Leigh's heritage.

Edna Hughes today 2013

Karen with brother Geoffrey

The Hughes and their neighbours were all re-housed by the council. Today Edna Hughes 87 years young, lives in a neat and welcoming bungalow in Westcliff on sea with all amenities , in such sharp contrast to her life in the 1950s/60s/

Karen Ratchford (nee Hughes)

The following is Karen's story of life in Old Leigh

As an adult I now realise that my memories of life in Leigh are in stark contrast to my mother's, who faced the reality of living in what was quite an impoverished area. For me it was a happy childhood with the freedom to roam and I loved my school days at North Street school , where I always came in the top three in my class. I was reminded of my humble background when I passed the eleven plus, when the father of another pupil remarked that he

was surprised I had succeeded, bearing in mind where I came from! (All of Karen's siblings did well and went on to good careers)

With my older brother Geoff , we used the beach, cliffs and Leigh Marshes as our playground. We would go "crabbing" at low tide, which our Dad frowned upon as he thought it was cruel. Over on the Marshes we would seek out slow worms and grass snakes by lifting up old pieces of corrugated iron. We also used to forage on the massive rubbish dump—I can still remember the smell today. Somehow we always seemed to find something of interest, my best find was a bendy Rupert toy in perfect condition. In those days there was no such thing as a boot sale, so unless items were taken to a jumble sale they were literally thrown away. Another pleasure was running up and down or bouncing on the planks leading up to the cockle boats, when they weren't being used to unload the day's catch. When the tide was out we would spend time digging in the creek where we would often come across old green bottles.

During the summer months the Old Town was transformed by the hoards of visitors, both local and from out of town. I used to befriend other children in the car park of the Peter Boat. I was fascinated to hear about their lives in London and other faraway places they had visited. My best friend was Hilary Dolby who lived at 74a High Street, which was the old Custom House. As you entered through the large doors at the front of the house, you were confronted by a wooden floored courtyard, to one side was the front door of 74a to the other was the entrance to 74b. The Dolby's house was much larger than mine, with a lovely lounge that had a fireplace at one end with shelving for ornaments. There was also a spacious dinning room, which had a dinning table and chairs and a large dresser. I clearly remember a selection of bag pipe and marching band records on the sideboard, which were a favourite of Hilary's dad Jim Dolby. His wife Brenda preferred the sound of the Walker Brothers! Hilary and I played for hours in the courtyard as children, out of harms way and not under her mothers feet. We had a toy tea set and held regular dolly tea parties, as well as putting on small plays for which we charged a small fee for people to watch. Then we would head off to Mr Thompsons the grocer to buy a bag of sweets. Jim Dolby was employed at Leigh railway station as a ticket collector. His wife Brenda worked for Stephen Ford making up ornamental dyed white weed displays, alongside my mother. Sadly both

Karen and her brother on the beach, in the background the old railway station.

Jim and Brenda died young and after marrying in her late teens Hilary emigrated to Australia. Another friend was Angela McKenzie who lived in the row of cottages directly opposite the Peter Boat car park I recall her family sometimes collected sea lavender and would sell bunches from their front room window.

My dad Stanley used to have a bicycle with a seat on the front, but later he brought a motorbike and sidecar and we would holiday every summer in Devon. My older brother would ride pillion, whilst my younger sister Debra and I

The Hughes family

would sit on the back seat of the side car with mum and baby brother Christopher in the front seat. All our luggage would somehow be stuffed in around us. Nearer to home during the summer we would enjoy boat trips on Snappy Noakes pleasure boat and some weekends Dad treated us to crisps and lemonade, with a bottle of milk stout for my Gran. I used to go to fetch it from the Crooked Billet, you climbed a few steps to a small hatch where you could order drinks without going in, the problem was I was to short to be seen and dad would have to come over and get us served. On Sundays a lovely old man would set up his weighing and measuring machine, it would cost a penny and every couple of months I would be weighed and measured. Sundays also meant that I attended Sunday school at the Leigh Road Methodist Church.

One year whilst going to school when it was very icy and frosty, I tried to walk up church steps but kept sliding back down. Mrs Cotgrove came along with her basket on wheels picked me up and popped me inside. She then took me all the way to the top. When I was nine years old the council condemned our property, the 1953 floods had ruined the fabric of the house and there were also sanitation problems as well. We were re-housed in Eastwood where there was a proper indoor toilet and bathroom and a lawn to the back and front of the house. We had only had a back yard in Leigh. For my Mum it must have been wonderful to have all these amenities which made her life so much easier. Although we no longer lived in the old town my Dad never really left as he was a member of the Leigh Motor Boat Club until he died.

For me I missed the sound of the waves lapping on the shore, the noise of the seagulls screeching above my head and the loss of my freedom to roam the beaches and surrounding area.

Karen has not forgotten her Leigh roots and visits the High Street on a regular basis, to eat in the cafes and walk her dogs with husband Richard. Today Karen is a volunteer at the Leigh Heritage Centre.

Karen's dad Stanley.

The Hughes' children having fun on the beach.

Karen's on Grandma Hughes' lap with sister Deborah.

Karen with Bell Wharf in the background.

Dad Stanley with Karen in his arms. Her grandma standing beside him.

© E Hughes

Tony Carr
A Noakes Connection

Contact with Tony Carr, revealed that his mother, Mary was a member of the Noakes' family. Her father was Thomas Alfred Noakes (1871–1929). At the time of Mary's birth in 1923, the family were living at no 2 Peter Boat Cottages, which flooded every spring tide, forcing them to move furniture upstairs. The cottages have since been demolished.

Thomas Noakes married twice, his first wife Ellen died in 1903, leaving him with three daughters to raise. In 1908 he re-married, his bride, Bertha Saphin (1885–1961) was the daughter of a watchmaker. Their first home together was in Prittlewell, where daughter Phyliss and son Harry were born. To support his family Thomas was a Carman Coal Merchant.

*This photograph was taken outside the
Peter Boat Public House.
Thonas Noakes, wearing a Bowler Hat.*
© T Carr

*Henry Peter Saphen (Bertha's
father) who was a watchmaker.*
© T Carr

*Bertha Noakes (wife of Tom)
standing at the front door of her
home. (No 2 Peter Boat Cottages)*
© T Carr

In 1911 Alfred was living with his family at number 5 Alley Dock, cottages behind the Peter Boat. They remained in the old town for many years.

Alley Dock.
By permission of Leigh Heritage Centre

Harry Noakes, in the foreground
working on the crane
on Alley Dock.
© T Carr

At the western end of Alley Dock there used to be a communal toilet which overhung the sea wall. At the eastern end of the cobbled alley, were stables for horses. These horses used to pull the wagon loads of goods from the wharves, up the hill for distribution inland. The alley was also the site of an early town jail.

Thomas and Bertha Noakes, 'Sanders'
grand children
© T Carr

The Clarkes

The Clarke family have a long history of living and working in Leigh. Jack Clark was a local fireman . Other members of the extended family had shops on The Broadway.

Charles Clark was the Chief Ranger of The Ancient Order of Foresters one of the many Friendly Societies at the time, seen here parading in front of a funeral possession in Leigh. The society used to meet at the Ship Public House, at the bottom of Leigh Hill.

Charles was also a member of the Essex Rifle Volunteers in the late 19th Century at the time of crisis with France.

In later years Charles Clark worked on the London to Leigh Railway.

By kind permission of David Hope

Bell Wharf

The railway sidings can be seen the background.

The town clerk reported that Bell Wharf would be closed to all commercial traffic on and after the 1st of July 1952.

The following year the Medical Officer for Health informed the council, that the existing drinking fountain on Bell Wharf be replaced by a modern type at the approximate cost of fourteen pounds. This was agreed.

A request was submitted to the relevant committee, by the Pier and Foreshore Manager, for the use of current office accommodation on Bell Wharf, to be converted to a refreshment kiosk. This request was refused as the building was due for demolition to enable vehicular access along the west to the wharf..

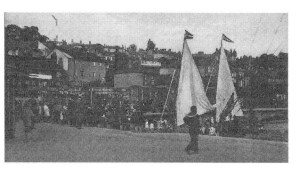

A busy day on Bell Wharf.

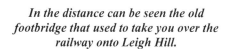

In the distance can be seen the old footbridge that used to take you over the railway onto Leigh Hill.

The Southend School of Art—Wednesday Group

Ivy Morse, front row first right. Behind her is a young Sheila Appleton
© *R Morse*

The art group was originally the idea of Neil Hardy a tutor at Southend College of Arts and Crafts. Wanting to encourage more people in the 1950s—in particular "housewives" (a term we would not use quite so readily today) to take up painting and sketching. With the quaint old fishing village offering such diverse material for budding artists, the group rented temporary accommodation on the High Street. The property owned by Southend Council was due for demolition so the art group were only allowed to use the ground floor. The group would later move a few doors along to Conduit House (still there today—called The Coal Hole). Not to be confused with the original Coal Hole Beer House. The group continued to meet into the 1960s.

Public Houses
Humble Beginnings

In Medieval times, alehouses were central to the life of any village or small town, where it was usually the women—known as ale wives—who brewed the ale for sale and consumption in the family home, which was often quite small and shabby. These beverages would only have been served to the common working man—labourers, cobblers, pedlars or servants. Occasionally travellers who required lodging for the night, would be afforded nothing more than bedding on the kitchen floor or in the barn. During the middle ages with increased population and industries polluting the drinking water, ale became the only safe way to quench your thirst. From the 14th century the alehouse became a little more sophisticated, with a sign hung outside to attract customers. with a room set aside for drinking only. Although most would have a given name, the hanging signs would have been mainly pictorial, as the majority of the population were illiterate. The alehouse during this period also began offering basic food to accompany their beverages, buns, bread and cakes and these establishments were now managed entirely by men. During the 18th century the ale house changed its title to—public house—but its customers were still the lower working classes.

Inns are thought to owe their origins to monks who offered the wayfarer or pilgrim, food, drink and a resting place for the night in their monastery. That was until Henry VIII ordered the dissolution of these and other religious buildings, between 1536–1541. Far from disappearing Inns continued to grow and flourish during the reign of his daughter Elizabeth 1st (1558–1603) but were now purely commercial enterprises in the hands of individual landlords. Here the wealthy and educated would gather to drink wine (as opposed to beer or ale) to converse and relax with their equals. Some of the larger inns offered cock fighting or plays to entertain their patrons. Decades later there would be coaching Inns, notable by the large archway leading into a courtyard, where the traveller would alight in order to enter the inn, leaving the horses to be fed, watered and rested for the next day's journey.

During the 19th and 20th century, landlords recognized the need for change, to suit a different kind of customer. Prior to the Second World War, skittles and dominoes were common pursuits for men to enjoy with their chosen beverage. The advent of the 1950s saw television and other leisure pursuits gradually become available to all and the social life of the average family took on a new direction. The publican could no longer take for granted that his premises would be full of customers each evening. One idea to attract more customers was offering food— previously only available from the bar—now served in an area specifically for those wishing to dine, as well as enjoy the beverage of their choice. This as we know today, is one feature that is extremely popular with the general public and in many cases has been instrumental in keeping pubs open. Quiz nights, dart teams, live bands and karaoke, also helped fill these establishments and have become common place, in public houses all over the country. There was one aspect of income that was lost to the publican, with the arrival of supermarkets in the 1970s and that was the sale of their wine, beer and spirits from their off sales counter. Not only did the supermarket undercut their prices, but with wine, beer and spirits readily available on the shelves, the discerning drinker no longer had to make that extra trip to the local pub to purchase their alcohol

Today the public house is far more family oriented, with bright carpets, comfortable seating and attractive lighting. In the 1990s the tradition of having frosted or smoked glass in their windows (previously used to obscure the clientele from the street) was replaced by clear glass. This made the interior of the premises brighter and far more inviting, adding to the new modern design of the local. When the ban on smoking was introduced, hundreds of public houses across England and Wales, ceased trading. Today there are still public houses to be found in the cities, towns and villages, offering food, drink and somewhere for the weary traveller or tourist to rest and partake of refreshments and a bite to eat.

The Old Town

The old town was served at different times by no less than ten drinking houses with many of the early pubs originally private dwellings. Today (2013) you will only find The Ship, Crooked Billet, Smack, The Peter Boat and the newly built public house, The Mayflower. In 1625 the Watermans Arms, originally a private residence was sited to the east of the Old Custom House—which today is private accommodation. By the 18th century the Watermans Arms had became a licensed house. Little evidence remains today of this

The Mayflower Public House (2012)

pub, except that by 1854 it was no longer known by that name and was said to have passed into the hands of William Foster and that parish meetings were held there on a regular basis. The Crown Inn, built in the 1550s also began life as a private house and remained so until the 17th century when it too was licensed to sell alcohol. This building stood, on what today is a small car park with a large gift shop on one side, the Old Custom House on the other. Embedded in the wall facing the car park of the Custom House, are the remains of an old fireplace, thought to have been part of the interior of the Crown Inn. For a number of generations (beginning with the reign of Elizabeth 1st) the house was owned by the Hare family, beginning with Captain Thomas Hare, it then passed to his son William, next came Samuel Hare a Barrister and JP. Eventually ownership passed out of the family and was bought

What little remains of The Crown (2012)

by Vigerius Edwards a barrister, next came a Mrs Herber. Researching this name only revealed a Reginald Heber b1854 at Leigh-on-Sea. The building was sold to the railway when the line came through the village but it was some considerable time before it was demolished.

The name given to any individual responsible for the day to day running of his or sometimes her pub, varied from—licensed victualler, landlord, licensee ,publican or simply the gaffer. Far from having the experience to take on such a role (today you would have a manager or a couple trained in every aspect of managing a public house, before they are allowed to be in charge) early publicans came from all walks of life, with no experience whatsoever. Experience or not, they would have had to apply for a licence to sell alcohol and with it would have come rules and regulations on running such an establishment. Break the rules, lose your licence. Staff were of course needed to serve the customer and keep the premises habitable. Usually this responsibility fell to the publicans wife and daughters, who would take on the task of cleaning and the role of barmaid. In Victorian times they would only have served in the lounge or saloon bar, where there would have been a better class of patron! There were of course also barmen. Cellar men were responsible for keeping the cellar well organised and for bringing up the barrels of beer to the bar. Pot men and pot boys, were employed to clear tables. Their original function was to wash the pewter mugs used for drinking in the days before glass was introduced. Now the drinker can view the contents served to him by the landlord before consuming.

The Ostler attended horses of the independent traveller or those that were used to pull the stage coaches. The Bell Inn was once a thriving destination for these stagecoaches on their way to London and would have kept the Ostler busy, as up to a dozen coaches would pull in on any given day. With the introduction of the motor car their role naturally disappeared. Today The Bell, although still standing at the bottom of Leigh Hill, having been moved from its prime position in the High Street, to make way for the railway, now stands forlorn and derelict. For those passing the building today it would be hard to imagine the importance this near ruin once played in Leigh-on-Sea's past. The following pages will show some of the history of the

remaining public houses, the breweries who owned them and the landlords and staff who worked there over the decades. For some there is scant information, others have strong and lasting connections with Old Leigh.

The Bell Hotel now derelict stands at the bottom of Leigh Hill. Once it occupied a prime position on the High Street but was demolished because of the railway.

United Brethren Beer House

The Old United Brethren Building today 2013.
Now private residences

The name would suggest a connection to religion or perhaps the Masons, but in this instance the use of the word "brethren" came about because two brothers, Charles Stanton Gray who was listed in 1841 as a Maltster and Brewer as was his brother Joseph Gray. It is thought that the brothers were brewing beer as early as 1828. The Gray family continued as brewers right up to the 1970's and in the very early days their first beer houses were known as The United Brethren (there is still a public house with this name in Chelmsford today) The one on the High Street Leigh on sea, was originally two cottages made of lathe and plaster frames, constructed in 1600. Richard Thorn a bricklayer who was living in the cottages in the 1840's, converted the two properties into a beer house, by joining the two houses together and bricking the front. Before his death in 1856 he conveyed the property to Wells and Perry, wine merchants and brewers, which would confirm he owned the building , that had originally sold the products of the Gray brothers. On his death in 1856, the certificate showed him to be a publican rather than a bricklayer. Richard Thorn was married twice and had eight children of whom four sons went on to become carpenters and joiners, daughter Elizabeth emigrated to New Zealand and son William to Australia…..

Following Richard Thorn's death in 1856, the new landlord was William Thompson (b 1821) in Leigh. He lived there with his wife and children until 1867. The premises were advertised during his stay as a beer and boarding house. Between 1867 -1871 Stephen Gusterson born in Rochford in 1841 was the landlord. He left to manage the United Brethren Beer house in Chelmsford. John Joseph Baker took over the Leigh establishment for the next four years, leaving in 1878. For the next twenty years George Dawson born in Prittlewell 1840 was to be the landlord, leaving in 1895. Again we have a gap with no clear idea of who was running the United Brethren until 1898 when Albert Arthur Brewer took over. Like his father, Albert was originally a butcher by trade, whilst other members of his extended family were shopkeepers in the Old Town. In 1902 Albert and his family moved to London where he was a coffee house keeper. He died in 1922. Ernest Percy Ball was the last landlord I could find details for, his time at the United Brethren was between 1905–1910.

Following the closure of the beer house the building was converted into two shops. Later the premises would become home to the Southend Engineering Works. Today the building has once again returned to its original use as a private residence..

Visitors to the High Street in the 1960s

©*Robert Morse*

Coal Hole Beer House

The Coal Hole used to stand next to the Crooked Billet

In the 1600s The Coal Hole was known as "Gilmans At The Pale" and the home of Sir Richard Haddock and later Admiral Nicholas Haddock in 1770. When it changed from private use to beer house is unknown. The Coal Hole used to stand near the Crooked Billet and opposite where today stands Osborne's Seafood Merchants. In 1847 the owner was listed as a W. H. Carter, the occupants were John Going, William Emery and Edward Turnnidge. Were they lodgers or joint innkeepers? This was unclear. There follows a distinct lack of information about who owned or was the tenant of the Coal Hole until 1867 when Henry Eaton was there as the Beer House keeper. His tenancy lasted until 1870 when William and Maria Parsons from Lambeth with their six children moved in. William had previously been a potter. The family returned to Lambeth in 1874 where he died soon after.

Tenants

1874–78	Charles Clipsham
1878–1882	James Wilson (1812–1896) originally from Cumberland. On his retirement with wife Maria he moved to South Benfleet where he later died.
1882–1890	Emma Smith. No further details available
1891–1898	Thomas Waters (1840) born in Wiltshire
1896-1899	James Miller Stevens b 1857 in Kent, his wife was a confectioner. The Stevens time as Innkeepers was just three years, although they remained in the area, James became a market gardener.
1900–1905	Walter Burchfield another Kent man, born in Birling 1864. The son of a blacksmith. Unmarried he was innkeeper for some 5 years. Previously he had been a mate on the vessel "Standard Kent"
1906–1909	James Mulley B 1866 Canvey Island. James and his wife Elizabeth had one son during their time at Leigh. Cyril John Patrick Mulley In 1905.

Why and when the building was demolished I have been unable to find any information. Today where the building once stood is a seating area part of the Crooked Billett public house.

A view of the area today where the Cole Hole Beer House used to stand now a seating area.
© *Barry Edwards*

As you come over the flyover and enter the Old Town you will see Osborne's Seafood Merchants
© *Barry Edwards*

The Smack Inn
New and Old

The Smack today. (2013)
© *B Edwards*

The original Smack Inn faced the Thames and like many of the habitats in the village, was lost to the railway, when purchased for demolition. Court rolls listed John Flowers, a Leigh mariner, as one of the owners of the house, who in the 1600s sold the property to Sarah Goodlad, daughter of John Bundocke. The Goodlad family continued to reside at the property for a generation or two. The house with its orchard and open ground opposite (where later the current Smack would be erected) would eventually be sold again to Doctor John Cook, who was part owner— there are no records to show who else owned a portion of the property. The exact date when the building became a licensed premises is not known but by the 19th Century it would certainly have been a public house, as evidence shows the building was purchased by Lambirth and English, Essex Brewers.

Brewers—Lambirth and English

Part of their business stood at Little Stambridge. Henry Lambirth and John English were related by marriage though Henry's wife Martha English, John's sister. Their partnership was formed in 1808 and would last until Henry's death in 1835. Lambirth was already a successful wine and spirit merchant, in his birthplace of Writtle, where he set up his original establishment in 1803. Henry and wife Martha had a daughter—Frances, who married an Alfred Joseph Hardcastle, in 1840, who like her father was the owner of a large brewery in Essex, as well as being a wine and spirit merchant. Alfred was also a Liberal member of Parliament between 1847–1855. As well as being Deputy Lieutenant for Surrey and Justice of the peace for Suffolk, Norfolk and Essex. When the railway came through (1850s) and the Smack had to be demolished it would be Alfred Joseph Hardcastle who would buy the Smack but far more important, was the parcel of land he purchased opposite (previously used for boat building) which came with the sale. Here would be constructed the new Smack, on the site it still occupy's today. Twenty years later Alfred's son Henry Hardcastle and Thomas Osborne would buy shares in the original Lambirth and English Brewery.

Luker and Co.

During the 1900s another brewery would take possession of the Smack, this time a local one, Luker and Co. based in Southend-on-Sea. Originally there were three Luker brothers from Oxfordshire who were in business together, but it would be Henry Luker who would be the most prominent and successful.

Landlords–Publicans–Licensed Victuallers–Innkeepers

John Fairchild followed by Samuel Fairchild were at the Smack between 1803–1839 William Elijah Wiseman was publican between 1839 until his death in Leigh 1842. The next occupant of the Smack was John Bayford, born in Great Burstead in 1809, who stayed for over 20 years. He arrived circa 1844 with wife Jane Fisher and daughter Lucy, born in Little Stambridge. From 1847–1858 his family grew, with the birth of four sons and another daughter, Alice. John Bayford left the Smack in 1870, but only to move to the Peter Boat where he died in 1875. Of his six children only three of his four sons remained in the area, Benjamin, who was a blacksmith on new Road, before moving with his wife Elizabeth Risby to Prittlewell, Essex, where he died in 1919. Son William b1852, stayed on the High Street with his family, earning a living as a labourer, along with brother Frederick 1855–1902 and his wife Sarah Murrell. Like his brother, Frederick worked as a labourer. Their remaining brother Henry 1849–1886 left the area and moved to London where he was a Furrier Corporal in the 2nd Lifeguards. Their sister Lucy moved to Romford where she married, leaving Alice the youngest of the Bayford's, to wed Henry William Stewart, a police sergeant who was stationed in Shoreditch, where the couple lived for many years.

John Bundock was the licensed victualler between 1870–74 originally a master shipwright he had travelled to Australia from his native Leigh, in the 1850s where his first two children were born. Returning to England, a further seven children were added to the family and were to be found living with their parents in Bell Cottages Leigh Hill in 1881. Here John Bundock died in 1888. The two publicans that followed him stayed only a short time and offered me limited information on their lives. Harriett Brion 1878–1881 and Henry S Bayon, born in Jamaica (British subject) 1881–1882.

In 1882 joint owners of the Smack were Henry Cotgrove and John Emery.

William Edward Robinson and his wife Emily Cotgrove, took on the Smack following the departure of Henry Bayon, staying until 1894. William had been a fishmonger living on Hamlet Road, in Southend, before embarking on his role as a publican, an occupation he returned to when he left the Smack. Following the Robinson family came Edgar White, his wife Harriett and son Edgar. Edgar senior, grew up with his mother and stepfather John Lilly, at the Cricketers Inn, London Road, where the couple managed the public house. Still there today, the Cricketers has served the locals for over 150 years. During the time that the White's lived in

Leigh they had two more children, Francis 1896, Ethel 1900. Edgar White moved back to Prittlewell where he ran The Park Hotel at 63 London Road. Into the Smack now came a name well know to the area.

Henry G Choppin

Henry George Choppin 1867–1940 born in Hadleigh, Essex, was the son of the businessman Henry Choppin 1841–1931. His father was the licensee of The Bell Hotel on Leigh Hill, The Pier Hotel Southend-on-Sea and was instrumental in building the Grand Hotel, Leigh. Henry George, moved out of the area in the 1890s to live and work as a barman in London. Here he met his future wife Rose Coote, they married in 1899 and the birth of their first child Thurza, followed a year later. By the time their daughter was just ten months old they were living at the Smack, thanks to Henry's father, who having heard the pub was looking for a new landlord arranged for his son, to become the licensee. A position he would hold until 1930. During their

Henry G Choppin, with his grand daughter His father Henry seated beside them. Standing is Henry G's daughter Thuza.
Courtesy R Cooper

years at the Smack four more daughters and one son were born. George Leonard Choppin, was delivered in the back bedroom of his parents pub in 1906. George would later be the licensee of The Golden Lion in Prittlewell. Elsie never married. Mable wed a Wilfred Grey, Doris became the wife of Daniel Lay and Ella Rose married Ralph Gilson Cooper (many of the photographs and other information on this page come courtesy of Roger Cooper).

On retirement in 1930 Henry George Choppin moved to 73 Somerville Gardens, Leigh, where on his death in 1940 he left to his wife Rose Ellen Choppin effects totalling £3610.4s.

Henry Choppin Senior
Courtesy R Cooper

May 1919 the Smack complied a souvenir booklet with their regular customer's comments on life in the pub. Unfortunately most were unsigned and we will never know who added their thoughts and poems to the publication. To follow are just a few of the entries:

No1
Of all the pubs I've across there's none to beat the Smack
Of all the publicans I know old George is hard to whack
He sometimes acts the giddy goat and comes it rather warm
But don't you take no notice for he doesn't mean no harm
No2
Now everyone knows Thurza—Queen of the Smack is she
You might to see her boss the show when father's on a spree
She's dainty and she's saucy she's our bright particular star
BUT
Keep your eye upon the measure when Thurza's in the bar.
No 3
Bill Lucking's in the corner, his elbow on the bar
With half a pint afore him and a big "tophole" cigar
Now Bill aint no chicken and he knows a thing or two
Don't try to argue with him you'll be sorry if you do

William Lucking
William Lucking born 1850 in Leigh, spent his whole life living on the High Street. First with his family (fishermen) later following his marriage he lived at No 22 and in 1911 was residing at No 68. His occupation given as labourer for Urban District Council.

No 4
Has anyone seen Stouty? Oh you'll find him right behind
Amongst the toffs and ladies and they treat him very kind
He knows the ropes does Stouty, there ain't no flies on im
And he's absolutely sober when he's full up to the brim
No 5
Now when you go into the Smack look out for lawyer Bill
You'll find him very handy if you wish to make a will
Or if you want to sell a house or buy a plot of land
He's ready to oblige you—and he's never underhand
No 5
Oh it's fine and comfy to watch Bawleys as they drift with ebb and flow
Its fine to watch the cargo boats and liners come and go
It's good to breathe the morning air and it's good to smell the sea
But it makes it all the better if there's whisky with your tea

Following Henry Choppin into the Smack, came Joseph and Martha Hames until 1940. No details as to who was the landlord after Hames but by 1950–1953 Captain Daniel Ford was the licensed victualler. Roy Hughes was there from 53–57. With changes of owners and suppliers it has been difficult to list all the later landlords into this public house. Today, having recently had a facelift the Smack is still in Old Leigh serving pints, not so much to local fishermen but to visitors and locals who choose to come into Old Leigh for a drink

Back row from left,
Henry G Choppin, Sam Shacleton, Charlie Bridge.
Front row, from left,
Mr Wilder, Benjamin Barnard, Harry Thompson.
Sitting in front,
Frederick Charles Kirby.
Courtesy R Cooper

The King's Head

The building which used to face west along Leigh High Street, was demolished in the early 1900s to provide an entrance and ticket office for the new railway station. Leigh Sailing Club now use the old building as their headquarters. In the Court Rolls of Leigh the Kings Head was formally mentioned as the "Hambro Merchant Arms" and then as the mansion and dwelling house of a George King, born in Leigh in 1863.

A Notable Character

In the early days of The Kings Head, Nathan Davey was both landlord and builder. Falling on hard times and with the bailiffs at the door, he successfully managed to get rid of them by feigning madness, pursuing them with a red hot poker. Nathan Davy also made coffins for the parish. Having received an order from Rochford, he duly fashioned the coffin and transported it over on his cart, only to discover the man was not dead!! On the journey home he became tired

Standing on this site today is Leigh Sailing Club

and knowing that the horse would find its own way home, tied the reins to the seat and laid down in the coffin to sleep, having first covered himself with the shroud. Passing through Eastwood a man seeing the horse going along by itself jumped up behind for a lift. On noticing the coffin with what appeared to be a corpse he soon leapt off in fright.

William Foster   1816–1900

The son of a shoemaker, William Foster was born in Witham, he would begin his new life and become a successful businessman by first being the licensed victualler at The Kings Head in 1839,which would remain under his control for the next twenty years. When he moved from the pub he lived first in New Road in a cottage then later built Pittington House nearby. Not content with just running the public house, he was also a coal merchant and an agent for Unity Fire and Life Assurance Associations added to this he was also a corn and flour dealer. The years brought success and money and he was able to buy land, on which he employed twelve men and eight boys. He also owned at one point, Hadleigh Ray, which he later sold to the Salvation Army for £4800. William was also a principle shareholder in the new gas works and a property and land developer. In April 1849, William Foster coal merchant was taken to the Rochford Petty Sessions for selling unjust weights of coal and fined 5s with costs of 9d.

Somewhat out of character, or so it would seem to me—perhaps someone employed by Mr Foster was not carrying out his duties as well as one might have expected.

With his new found wealth William Foster did not forget the less fortunate in the area and he served as the first chairman of the parish council and was described in the Chelmsford Chronicle in 1895 as "a tall upright gentleman, full of vigour, of broad intellect and mind that grasps the point in view". For thirty years he was the guardian of the poor. In 1876 William was awarded a medal from the Royal Humane Society for saving four people from drowning in the creek. On receiving his medal William Foster said "I am surprised, happy but very proud to receive this honour".

William Foster married twice but had no issue of his own, when he married for the second time, his new wife came with children and William adopted them. In 1900 he died aged 84 years, having led an interesting and industrious life as well as being a great benefactor to Leigh-on-Sea. All from humble beginnings as the landlord of The King's Head.

Tenants and Innkeepers

William Brazier 1828/9 John Bell 1832/34 who was also a barge owner. William Foster 1839-1855 (details above) Richard Phillips from West Ham, was landlord from 1871-1874 his son Frederick took over for three years before the arrival of Alexander Palmer, a Londoner born there in 1835. During the Palmers time at The Kings Head his two sons were born. The 1881 census showed that Alexander Palmer still living in Leigh, had given up being a publican and was now a signal fitter for the railway. The next publicans into The Kings Head came and stayed for some fourteen years, Daniel Osborne and wife Caroline Barnard (daughter of George Barnard) were resident with their four children until 1895. They were next to be found on the 1901 census at The Woodcutters Arms Eastwood, Essex.

The King's Head was lost to the demands of the railway, when the original station at Leigh could not cope with demand. A larger station was constructed (the original building is now the headquarters of Leigh Sailing Club).

Crooked Billet

The Crooked Billet is the only public House on the High Street today, not to have been named after a fishing boat. The definition of the word billet has various meanings—quarters for soldiers—thick piece of firewood, a metal bar (short roll inserted at intervals into a hollow moulding) or a boomerang shaped tree branch. It is widely believed that the tree branch is where the name comes from. Originally a private dwelling, built in the 1700s, as home to one Sir Richard Haddock. By the 1800s the building was licensed to sell beer and later other alcoholic beverages. At first the Billet was more of a Beer house and it would later transfer this licence to the Coal Hole, which stood adjacent to the pub. Both would continue to sell liquor. The original Billet has over the decades been extended and altered to such an extent , that not a great deal remains of the original property. During November 1853 a meeting was held in the pub and "The Billet Club" was formed. For reasons not explained, the legal name of the club was "The United Brethren!"

As with many drinking establishments of the time the men or on occasion women, who were resident at The Crooked Billet, were a mixture of those who spent a lifetime working as publicans around the country, or those who simply used it as a way of employment and accommodation for a short period, between earning their living in a variety of ways. Jane Cook was landlady for a year or two in the early 1830s. Jane was the first of only three women to be the landlady.

The Crooked Billet on the left of the picture.

1800s
Henry Frost

Born, Leigh 1812 the son of William Frost and Mary Cotgrove. Henry came to the Billet around 1839, staying nine years. Having lost his first wife Jane, during his time in the Crooked Billet, he was later to remarry and move to Prittlewell, where he was listed on the 1851 census as an unemployed licensed victualler. He chose not to return to a publicans life, instead he found work as a brickmaker. His son Henry (b1835) stayed in Leigh, following the more tradition family path, by becoming a fisherman, taking lodging for a time at The Peter Boat.

William Ralph Hay

Another local man, born around the same time as Henry Frost which makes it quite likely they knew one another, was William Ralph Hay. Although born in Leigh and christened at St Clements, he had left the old town moving up to Shenfield, in the early 1840's where he had a grocers shop. Returning to his birth place around 1848, he moved into the Crooked Billet with his wife and children, and was listed as the Victualler and a Van Proprietor! Also resident was his mother Mary Hay, and nearby on Leigh Hill lived his brother John, a fisherman. The Hay's only stayed until the late 1850s when they moved up to Bethnal Green where William was working as a Carman. His wife died shortly after they arrived in London, but he stayed on in the area and later remarried, dying in Bethnal Green in 1889.

Isaac Watts

A Thundersley man, born b 1816, The Drovers Arms in Rochford was his first public House before taking over the Crooked Billet in the 1850's. With him was wife Mary and her brother George Thomas, shown at the tender age of 33 to be a "Chelsea Pensioner". Also lodging on the premises were two agricultural labourers, George Webb and Thomas King. A third resident, was Jonathon Going a fisherman. Isaac Watts died in 1865 and for the next two years his wife Mary was the second woman to be the Innkeeper or landlady at the pub.

John Bull and Charles Andrews

These two gentleman stayed only a few years. John Bull four years, Charles Andrews three. John Bull b1829 came from South Ockenden, worked first as a labourer, before moving into the Crooked Billet, with his wife Charlotte and their niece Clare, who they raised as their own. John Bull was the Innkeeper between 1870–74, following their time at Leigh, the family moved to Wickford, where Charles was again an Innkeeper. By 1901, John Bull had returned to working on the land.. I have no information for Charles Andrews other than the fact he was at the Billet for just three years.

Robert Noakes

Another local man, with fishing connections. The son of John and Susan Noakes, Robert was born in 1848 and like his father worked first as a fisherman before becoming the landlord of the Crooked Billet in 1880. He managed the pub with his sister, but Emma passed away in 1884, followed by Robert in 1888.

Mark Henry Osband

Following the death of Robert Noakes came Mark Osband he stayed until 1891. Previously a labourer from Orsett, where he was born in 1864, he would turn his hand to several occupations during his working life. After his time in Leigh, he moved on to be the landlord of The Bull in Hockley, but didn't stay long before he became a general labourer in the same area. A move to London a few years later, found him during the 1920s running a tobacconists.

Ephraim Williams

For two decades, Ephraim Williams was a domestic gardener, first at Black Notley, Essex moving on to Vange, again in Essex. Son of a labourer, he was like the previous publican, born in Orsett around 1836. From domestic gardener, to publican is quite a change, but this seemed to be quite common in that age, when it appears anyone could take on the running of a public house. With his wife Emma and two daughters, all of whom helped him with the daily running of the Crooked Billet, until Emphraim's death in 1900. Emma Williams his widow would continue as innkeeper, for the next three years.

William Henry Theobald

The son of Henry James Theobald and Mary Everitt, who were farmers on nearby Belton Hills, William was born in Leigh 1871. He never married and for the most part lived and worked on the land owned by the family, as well as being a barge owner. William was licensed Victualler at the Crooked Billet, for just three years. He remained in Leigh until his death in 1944.

William Osborne

Into the Billet now came an Osborne and there would be a member of this family resident, for the next 31 years. William Osborne (1858–1934) became the publican in 1907 with his spouse Mary Amelia (a case of intermarrying as his wife was also an Osborne). Previously he had been a fisherman, but his grandfather Daniel had at one time been the landlord of The Kings Head. His grandson stayed at the Crooked Billet until 1933 when one of his sons Walter Osborne (1888–1967) took over the pub. Walter Osborne and wife Rose Turnnidge, daughter of David Turnnidge and Mary Meddle continued to run the Crooked Billett into the 1960s. By this time the pub occupied both number 50 and 51 The High Street .

Richard Belton
Born in the Crooked Billet

Through a meeting with Richard Baxter, who put me in touch with Diane Belton whose father Richard, along with his brothers and sisters were born in the Crooked Billet. As well as information there followed a delightful selection of family photographs,

A young Doris Osborne and Benjamin Belton
© *Belton Family*

The children of Doris Osborne and Benjamin Belton came to be born in The Billet, when their mother as a young women, moved into the public house, to help look after her uncles children, following the death of his wife. Previously Doris had lived next door at number 50, with her parents, Daniel (a fisherman) and Lillian Osborne along with her five siblings. Staying on in the public house, after her cousins had grown up, Doris would marry Benjamin Belton in 1927 and raise her own family in the Crooked Billet until 1939.

Richard was born first in 1928, followed by brother Peter, then sisters, Lillian, Olive and Jean. Finally along came brother John in 1936. Life for the older siblings, was spent growing up in Old Leigh, mixing with the fishing families and the freedom to roam the local area. The .Beltons moved from Leigh during the Second World War.

With so much known and written about the Osborne's of Leigh, I decided to give space to the story of Benjamin Belton and his family.

Born in Great Wakering 1896, Robert's grandfather Benjamin, drowned, six months before his son-Benjamin was born 1866. This left his pregnant wife Rose, with two daughters and another son. Emily Rose b1888, married in Rochford 1917 to a Murray Buckingham. Clara Ellen b 1890, never married nor did Charles Israel b 1894. 1911 Charles was employed as a sweet shop assistant in South Ockendon. Rose Belton re-married to a Frederick Crampin in 1902 and was still resident in

From the left Peter, John, and Richard Belton
© *Belton Family*

Great Wakering where Benjamin living with them, was earning his living as a gardener. With the outbreak of World War One he joined the Lincolnshire Regiment , which is the area the Beltons originated from. They are thought to have settled on Foulness, Essex around 1777.

I do not have any details of how Benjamin Belton and his future wife Doris Osborne came to meet. Today their son Robert in his eighties is living with his family in Australia.

The Osborne's

These are the children of Daniel and Lillian Osborne.
Bobby, Archie, Gordon, Madge, Bert, Doris and Stanley.
© *Belton Family*

A young Doris Osborne
© *Belton Family*

Doris and Benjamin Belton
© *Belton Family*

*Richard Belton enjoying a pint
in the Crooked Billet, June 2012*
© *Belton Family*

*L—R Teddy Cotgrove, Richard
Belton, Joey Deal, Eddie Dentch and
seated Bobby Osborne,
Richard's cousin*
© *Belton Family*

*Diane Belton celebrating her 55th birthday
Crooked Billet 2012.*
© *Belton Family*

*Doris Belton, Hendrika and
Richard Belton 1980.*
© *Belton Family*

The Peter Boat Inn

Occupying the largest area for a public house in the Old Town today, is the Peter Boat, although this was not always the case during the buildings early years when it was known as the Peter Boat Inn. Visit today for or a meal or drink and you will find a car park and large outdoor seating area, where once there was a terraced row of houses and shops. Like so many buildings on the High Street they were demolished as being unfit for human habitation or simply stood in the way of progress. More fortunate, but not entirely, the terrace on the other

The buildings on the left of the photograph next to the Peter Boat were demolished a number of years ago.

side of the public house, known today as Reginald and Theobald Cottages, were re-built after a fire in 1892. This was the year the landlord, Richard Stammers, is said to have tripped on the stairs, dropped his lantern and the Peter Boat built of just lathe and plaster was soon ablaze, the fire spreading to the cottages next door. All were razed to the ground as was the pub. On being re-built the old wooden cottages and The Peter Boat, were constructed of studier materials, bricks and mortar.

In keeping with other drinking establishments on the High Street, The Peter Boat was formally a private residence. Records provided by the archivists team at Leigh Heritage Centre, show the building was constructed in the 1600s. The first available information on who lived there, were noted as a Mary and John Pulley, who would later surrender the tenement to one Samuel Osborne. He died in 1695 leaving the property to his son John. Ownership then missed a generation when John Osborne left the house to his grandson–another John, who is credited with converting the building into a public house, around 1739. By 1758, John Osborne still the owner, had as a tenant, John Wright, a Rochford

Theobald and Reginald Cottages (2013)

Maltster, who was resident for about two years. Mathew Yaxley a Leigh baker followed (landlords or publicans often had other occupations) and remained in situ for a 20 year period up to 1773. By this time Ann Osborne was listed as The Peter Boats owner. Between 1828/9 John

Fairchild was landlord and from 1830/9 James Hills. Following James Hills came Arthur Hay, a local butcher, who was the publican from around 1840, giving up the tenancy within five years. Moving out of the pub he took a cottage on Leigh Hill with his wife and children, were he continued to be a butcher. The next family into the pub were the Utton's whose name would not be so much associated with the Peter Boat but with the local brickfields and house building.

The Uttons

John Utton came from Suffolk, where he was born in 1796, at some point he came to Leigh-on-Sea, where he married local girl Isabella Emery in 1835. They rented a cottage on Leigh Hill and during this period of his life, John was a general labourer. By 1845 John and Isabella and three of their children took over the Peter Boat, where they stayed until the 1850s. After which John is shown as a beer house keeper, further along the High Street, at Exhibition House (as a number was not given I am unable to say exactly where the building stood). In 1871 John Utton died and it was from this point his son—John who was a bricklayer left Leigh and moved with his wife to West Street, Prittlewell, to number one Utton Villa. From this point on John (1836–1894) prospered and was soon employing up to twenty men. The Utton's extended family continued in the business expanding into house building around the Southend area, including seven properties on Utton Avenue, Leigh. The bottom of this Avenue comes out onto New Road, which runs parallel with the railway line, opposite the Old Town, where it all began with John Utton seniors time in The Peter Boat Inn.

Descendants of the Utton family remain in the town. Sheila Utton, was a local school teacher, who married James Clinckscales, who was a Southend Councillor for a number of years.

A Local Landlord or Two

The Peter Boat had as landlord between the 1850s until the late 1860s, a local man, Thomas Robinson. Again, as well as being landlord he was a fisherman/fishmonger. Thomas and his wife Jane, later moved to Grays, Thurrock. They opened a fishmongers on the High Street where they traded for the next twenty years. John Bayford, previously in The Smack, took over after the Robinsons, until his death in 1875. John was also a coal merchant. An Osborne was now back running The Peter Boat from approximately 1875–1880 and again in 1887–1891. During these two periods, Josiah Osborne b1825, the son of a local farmer, was in charge, in between time he was to be found working on the land. On the occasions Josiah was not being a publican, Henry Ellis Surridge was the landlord.

Henry Ellis Surridge

Like his wife Elizabeth Surridge (they were cousins) Henry Ellis Surridge was born in Leigh (1831–1899). As a young boy he was an apprenticed barge builder, in Lime Street, London. Following his marriage in 1858, having completed his apprenticeship he continued building barges. Quite why he gave it up and became a licensed victualler in London during the 1870s, is not known. By 1880, with his wife, he was back in Leigh, running the Peter Boat, staying seven years. With the couple were their daughters, Eliza, Emma and Annie, plus two lodgers, the Bayford brothers (sons of John) of whom one was a coal merchant. 1891 saw the death of Elizabeth, the family were no longer at the Peter Boat, but living in a cottage still on the High Street. Henry was now a carpenter, his daughters were dressmakers. Henry Surridge died in 1899 and at this point Eliza and Annie, moved to Avenue Road, Leigh where they become house keepers. Eliza died 1942, Emma 1944 and Annie the youngest 1952.

1980s

Josiah Osborne returned to the pub until around 1886, until Richard Stammers took over in 1891, where he was shown as the inn keeper of The Peter Boat. Born in Tillingham Essex 1835, Richard married Hannah Barrell in Maldon 1854, where their first daughter was born. A move to South Benfleet, Essex, where Richard had employment as a bargeman, saw the birth of another girl. Their last two children, a son Walter and a third daughter came during the Stammer's time in Fobbing, Essex. 1881 no longer a bargeman, Richard Stammers was now a farmer of 125 acres. Within ten years a move to Leigh-on-Sea at the grand old age of 60, Richard Stammers was the innkeeper of the Peter Boat (he is alleged to have accidently set fire to the place). Retiring in 1901, he moved to Orsett, Essex where he died in 1904. With Richard Stammers retirement in 1901 came Ephraim Steward, a Wakering man (b1870) and his wife Annie Eliza Cotgtove. In 1891 Annie was working in the Sutton Arms public house in Southend, where Ephraim was living at the time, working as a house painter. Perhaps it was Annie wanting to return to Leigh and her experience of working in a pub, that led the couple to take on the Peter Boat. They enjoyed a ten years tenancy, before returning to Southend, where Ephraim Steward resumed work as a decorator.

During the year 1908, a request was submitted to Southend Borough Engineers for alterations to be made at The Peter Boat Inn, by owners H Luker and Co (Southend Brewery). When they became the owners of the property is not recorded. Luker's also owned The Smack during the same period.

Arthur Deacon

Originally from Birmingham (b1856) his early occupation had been as a cycle tool maker. During the years 1880–1898 he was married with four children His wife was to die in 1898, when his youngest child was just thirteen years of age. In 1901, Arthur had moved to Chelmsford (none of his children are with him) and we find him still a tool maker. He is lodging with a Robert and Susan Tuck and their spinster daughter Annie. Arthur and Annie married in 1902 and their son Harry William was born two years later. Following Robert Tuck's death the couple, with son and Roberts widow move to Leigh and the Peter Boat around

1908. They stayed for six years before vacating the premises, allowing Frank Stark to be the next licensed victualler.

Frank Horace Stark

Coming from three generations of carpenters, stretching back to his grandfather in Devon, Frank Stark naturally followed the family tradition and worked as a furniture maker in London , where he was born in 1884. He was still living in the capital in the early 1900's with his mother, who was now a widow. By 1911 he had moved to Essex and given up his trade, to be the manager of the Railway Hotel in East Street (still there). The following year he married Cecisly Woods and in 1913 their daughter was born. His wife had been a barmaid at the Horse and Groom in Rochford, where her father Oliver Woods was the publican. They moved into the Peter Boat 1914 and with their combined experience of working in public houses were an ideal couple to take on this old Leigh pub. They stayed until Frank Starks death in 1935, his wife died the following year. Their daughter remained in the area, marrying a Reginald Lewis in 1937

From 1937 until the 1950s, Leonard Williams and his wife Ida were managing The Peter Boat. Their daughter Sari was for many years a local hairdresser, still lives locally. Following the Williams came C K Mayo 1957–1968, previously the landlord of the Anchor Inn Canewdon.

In later years up to the current time, The Peter Boat has been owned and managed by various companies or large breweries, as opposed to local families or individuals.

2013
© *Barry Edwards*

Steaming Through

A brochure in 1908 described the railway facilities at Leigh on Sea thus:

> *Leigh is served by the Tilbury and Southend Railway*
> *Company and though there is talk of additional railway*
> *accommodation, as yet there is no competitor in this*
> *field. The railway station is at the foot of the hill, in*
> *the midst of the old town, which hardly gives an idea of*
> *what Leigh really is. In fact the station and its*
> *surroundings are apt to give visitors wrong impressions*
> *and so do injustice and harm to the town. But whatever*
> *the faults of the station and its site, there is nothing but praise*
> *can be given to the company's service of trains.*

The writer went on to list the service and times offered by the railway each day (except Sunday) fast trains and expresses that ran from 7am to 1pm to the city. With the same service being offered from London to Leigh. The journey taking no more than fifty minutes, with passengers seated in carriages that were comfortable and heated in the winter. The cost of a season ticket to second class passengers for the whole year was £14. This was extraordinarily cheap as it worked out at just 10d per day. The magazine further described:

> *Beginning at 4pm and continuing at frequent intervals ,*
> *a series of quick trains bring the jaded City man with little*
> *delay to the invigorating sea air of Leigh. For the theatre*
> *lover, his return can wait until midnight at which hour a*
> *train is waiting to take him from the smoke to the ozone.*

Early Days

The complexities of early railways, with numbers of small companies springing up all over the country, eager to invest in this modern from of transportation which offered fast travel for goods and passengers. During the 1840s there was a mixture of branch lines, with the occasional larger company laying track covering a hundred miles or more. Many of the early companies went bankrupt.

Proposals for a railway from London to the Essex seaside, were first considered in 1835, when a meeting was held at the Royal Hotel at the top of Pier Hill, Southend-on-Sea. The company authorised to carry out the work was the Southend and Hole Haven Railway. Following initial discussions, interest petered out and it would be left until the formation of the London Tilbury and Southend Railway Company, (formed in 1840) who would begin work in earnest in the

1850s, buying up land and laying track, to take the train down the line from Fenchurch Street to the seaside. This journey was far from straight forward, as the company went first to Tilbury, then Forest Gate and Barking before finally heading down to the coast. The original plan had been to take the final track miles along the seafront, with a terminus by Southend Pier. This met with stiff opposition from the residents living above in Royal Terrace, who complained, "the noise and smoke would be most disagreeable". Today Southend Central Station is located in the High Street and only two stretches of

Royal Terrace today 2013

track are really close to the Thames. Leigh-on-Sea and Chalkwell, both within walking distance of the beach.

Once completed the railway offered speedy transport to London. The fishing industry were the first to see the potential and began transporting tons of oysters, winkles, shrimps and mussels to the capital. They now reached their destination in just over the hour allowing the produce to arrive at market as fresh as it left the coast.

The arrival of the railway and its intent on splitting the village in half, must have caused enormous upheaval and uncertainty as to the future of the fishing village. With the majority of housing tenanted, the occupants would not have had any say in the loss of their gardens, or the property being demolished. Far from their homes being picturesque many of the residents on the High Street, lived in hovels unfit for human habitation. Thanks to the railway displaced families were re-housed in more sanitary dwellings, improving their living conditions. For those fortunate enough to be moved into new accommodation, the railways arrival had a positive effect. Those unaffected by these changes, their homes remained the same poor housing they had lived in prior to the arrival of the LTS. The owners of any properties or land taken by the railway were compensated for their loss. The same could be said for the powerful breweries who owned the public houses on the High Street. Whereas most were happy to settle for a sum of money for the loss of their properties and income, not all were prepared to give up without a fight.

Wells and Perry

The Bell Inn (now on Leigh Hill) once occupied a prime position in the village, unfortunately this was directly in the path chosen by the railway. The Inn was one of many owned across the county by William Collings Wells and Isaac Perry, Brewers and Wine Merchants, of Chelmsford. In 1852 they challenged the London Tilbury and Southend Extension Railway Act, by their putting objections before Parliament in a bid to save The Bell from being demolished. The petition failed, the building was lost, but they received £1800 for the land on which the inn had stood. The railway also agreed to a rather strange request to leave the front rooms standing to allow their tenant to continue business, until the new Bell Inn was constructed. A further request by the brewery, was for a level crossing to be made at the bottom of Leigh Hill, to allow the brewers free access to their wharf opposite. The LTS also agreed to pay £40 towards expenses incurred by the company having to purchase land on which to build their new inn. Wells and Perry also owned a timber yard, cottages, builders and a shop in the fishing village.

Wesleyan Chapel

The chapel was central to the life of the fisherman, taken down in the name of progress. In 1854 notice was given of "the intention to take and use the said building and in compensation the said company to build another chapel, superior to the present one". Unfortunately this proved not to be the case, such was the poor workmanship that the chapel had to be rebuilt. Today this building still stands on New Road, facing the railway that caused the original building to be demolished.

Wesleyan Chapel
1900s

Crossing the Track

With track laid through the heart of the town, access to St Clements Church and beyond, was now only possible by using one of the three level crossings. The largest and only one suitable for those with horses, carts and later motor cars, stood at the bottom of Leigh Hill and continued to serve the town until the 1960s. Originally this area was the market place, where each year on the second Tuesday of May was held the Leigh Fair. Those taking part paid the Lord of the Manor 3d, per foot frontage on their stalls for the privilege of selling their wares.

James Adams Gatekeeper standing at gate

Pedestrians were able to use one of the three footbridges over the line, one near Bell Wharf, another which spanned the main level crossing the third which today is behind Sarah's Tearooms.

Isaac Spurgeon is standing in front of a typical platelayers hut at the bottom of Billet Lane where he was level crossing keeper. The hut had a small coal stove to boil water for tea and warmth in the winter. Sometimes local children would put an old wet sack over the chimney to smoke him out.

© *R Craness*

The railway complete a workforce was needed to maintain the track, drive the locomotives and man the stations. I have found some of those whose job it was to keep the trains running and their passengers taken care off at their new station at Leigh-on-Sea, until it was moved in 1932. Now standing at the bottom of Belton Hills, the current station is still taking the locals to and from the city.

Gatekeepers

I cannot find any evidence of a gate keeper, prior to that of James Adams, who was the gatekeeper at this level crossing for over thirty years, until his death in 1905. Born in Drome Ireland in 1830, he left home to enlist in the army as a young man. He was to be found with his brother George, at the Garrison Barracks West Thurrock, in 1861 where the brothers served as artillery gunners. Marriage and three children followed this date, as well as completing his time in the army. Having moved to Leigh-on-Sea he swopped a military uniform for that of a railway employee. For many years the family lived on New Road. Following his death they all left the area, his widow Emma and unmarried daughter Rosetta, moving to West Ham.

From Platelayer to Gate Keeper–Isaac Spurgeon

Isaac Spurgeon had been a platelayer for twenty years, he was born In Mayland Essex in 1855, working first as a labourer in his home village. The 1881 census shows him lodging at Hill Cottage Leigh, with an Ernest Speller and his family, who all came from the same village as Isaac. Ernest was also earning a living as a platelayer. Although married Isaac's wife and baby son George were living with relatives in Fobbing, where later his daughter Emma would be born. His family would join him in Leigh around the time his daughter Alice was born in 1885 and the family were living in a cottage on Belton Way. Three more children followed Edith, Ernest and Thomas who arrived in 1890.

Isaac gave up working on the railway around 1899, to become the licensed victualler of the Plough and Sail at Hanningfield. The family story goes, that he had won the pub in a game of cards! Unfortunately in 1902 it was reported in the Essex Newsman that:

Isaac Spurgeon licensed victualler of East Hanningfield
pleaded guilty to being drunk on his own premises

Subsequently he sold the public house and returned to Leigh and employment on the railway.

In all I was contacted by three of Isaac Spurgeon's great grandchildren, all of whom have remained in the area. The first was Robert Cranness, then Dave Spurgeon who used to be a fisherman and owner of the Endeavour, which he sold in 1979. Today he is one of the trustees of the boat which has been restored to its former glory. "My father" he told me "was a master carpenter who during the last war had worked for Johnson and Jago". The last of these Spurgeon descendants was another Dave, this time David Lash Spurgeon who brought me a newspaper cutting of his great grandparents Isaac and Mary's golden wedding the report in 1928 went as follows:

David Lash Spurgeon

Dave Spurgeon

Mr and Mrs Spurgeon forty four years residents of Leigh -on-Sea celebrated their golden wedding on Friday. Both continue to enjoy good health. Two years before their wedding at St Michael's church in Fobbing, Mr Spurgeon entered the service of the old London Tilbury and Southend Railway Company, when they were working on the permanent way at Vange. Apart from a short break from the railway held continuous service at Leigh-on-Sea (even working on Sundays as he was not a religious man). On the 11th of November 1904 he was the first of old employees of the company to be made gatekeeper on the system and his wife still treasures the letter he received informing him that "in consideration of your long service your application to be appointed gateman to the Billett crossing has been sanctioned.—a position he held until 1925.

MR. and MRS. SPURGEON, of Leigh, who celebrate their Golden Wedding on Friday. (21.)

Also in the article, Mr Spurgeon recalled that in July 1888 after his transfer to Leigh, there was such a rough period of weather accompanied by floods, that trains could reach no further than Barking. Now fully retired Isaac Spurgeon named gardening as his favourite hobby and said he was particularly keen on cultivating vegetables of which he was something of an authority. Isaac Spurgeon died in 1932.

Another view of the level crossing, in the distance the shop run by Mrs Cobley

The Cobleys

Looking through the level crossing you can just make out the confectioners and post office, with the name "Cobley" above the door. The business was run by a Percy and Gwendolyn Cobley, who married in West Ham at the end of the First World War. Percy Walter Cobley (b1891) had served in the Royal Flying Corps. They moved to Leigh where they took over the shop and here their only child Pamela was born in 1922. Life was not to be kind to Gwendolyn (b1896) as her husband died in 1928 and ten years later their daughter (who was unmarried) passed away. Carrying on alone she was to remain in the shop until her retirement in 1970, continuing to live in the area Gwendolyn Cobley was 86 years old when she died in 1982.

Platelayers

The term platelayer was derived from the name of the track that was laid in the early development of railways, called "plateways" these were L shaped rails, used mainly by coal wagons. With the coming of passenger and goods trains, which were much heavier, new types of rail were needed, but the men laying this new track were still called platelayers. Once their work was completed, they were expected to maintain the track in good order with individual platelayers given 2–3 miles to patrol ensuring safe passage for the steam trains. Their base and shelter would be a small brick hut by the railway line.

The original doors to the station platform.

Platelayers were local men, but in the main they were outsiders, who would maintain the track through and around Leigh-on-Sea. The following names are just a few examples of the workforce, many of whom worked on the railway for twenty years or more.

1860s
Joseph Cox   b. 1826 Benfleet
John Heckford   b. 1829 Pitsea
Daniel Everett–Burch   b. 1829 Essex.

1870s–1900s
William Ellis   b1832 Leigh-on-Sea
lived at number 64 High Street for
12 years

The original station clock now in the Leigh Sailing Club.

Alfred Pudney	b 1830 West Tilbury
	his last child was born in Leigh in 1870.
William Bond	b 1867 Runwell
James Harvey	b 1865 Essex
	(boarding with John and Jane Going on New Road)
Henry Clark	b 1858 Upminster
James Skinner	b 1855 Essex
Henry Pond	b 1862 Essex
	Like J Harvey boarding at a house on New Road
William Knight	b 1857 Essex—residence 34 High Street

In the 1880s Edward and George Smith from Stanford-le-Hope were living at a lodging house

This is the original station for the up-line at Leigh-on-Sea which stood opposite to where the Smack Inn stands today.

on the High Street, run by Eliza Cotgrove a young Widow. Edward was 14 his brother only 13, but both were working as platelayers. In 1889 Edward married a girl from Hadleigh Essex and they moved to West Ham, where Edward still with the railway, was now a porter. George went on to be a signalman at Thurrock.

Also lodging with Eliza Cotgrove were Henry Turnidge b.1866 Ockenden Essex and Edward Houting from Stanford-le-Hope. Both platelayers.

Alfred Bishop came from Sutton in Essex, b. 1867, his father John was also a platelayer. By 1891, Alfred had spent a number of years working at Leigh, he later moved to Stanford-le-Hope where he continued to work on the railway. Nearer to home, William Partridge b1862 Leigh-on-Sea was a platelayer for over twenty years—from around 1880. Home for William in the early years was on the High Street. Following his marriage to Priscilla Wilder, the couple lived at number 22 New Road for a number of years.

Railway Signalmen

The responsibilities of a signalman was to operate points and signals from the signal box. He was also expected to check the train as it passed by, in order to see the red light that would hang from the last carriage. This would confirm that the train was complete and the section clear. Each train movement was logged in a giant ledger, which rested on its own table as it was too heavy and cumbersome to be moved.

Frederick James Cotgrove, born Leigh-on-Sea 1864, was first a fisherman before becoming a railway employee. In the 1890s he was employed as a porter but was promoted to signalman by 1901, he continued in this position for the next ten years.

The new railway station 1910. To the right buildings on Leigh Hill now demolished. In the distance the footbridge over the main level crossing . Just past the footbridge can be seen the station for the down line backing onto New Road.

Walter Edmund Taverner from Feering in Essex, was living in Bell Cottages in the 1880s. He was employed as a signalman but his service was sort lived as he was only 35 when he died.

Mark Moses b. 1881 in Essex, resided on Joscelyne Square around 1911, having come from Grays Station where he had a duel role as porter/signalman.

In the 1890s William Reeve Law from Hadleigh and Henry Archer born in 1868 in Hertfordshire were signal men at Leigh in 1891. William married Julia Maud Ransley, daughter of a Leigh police constable. The couple moved first to Thurrock, and then in 1913 were living at Tilbury, where William still worked for the railway. For Henry Archer, his service was much shorter, a few years later he is working as parcel courier in Deptford. He died in 1945 back in Hertfordshire .

The Station

This large brick building, replaced the original station. The building today (2013) is now the headquarters of Leigh Sailing Club.
© *Barry Edwards*

When first opened in 1855/6 Leigh Railway Station had an entrance for the down line on New Road. Opposite, access to the platform for the up line came from the middle of the High Street. This arrangement continued for nearly thirty years until conditions became cramped and expansion was needed for that section of the station. With no available space it was necessary to build a completely new station and booking office at the site most people associate with the Old Leigh Station. This was at the bottom of Leigh Hill on the other side of the old level crossing. The building was completed in 1910 and resulted in the demolition of the King's Head Public House.

Attached to the original Leigh station in the late 1860s was Wardell and Rackshaws Salt and Coal Company. This partnership ended with the following announcement in the London Gazette October 4th 1870.

> *Notice is hereby given that the partnership subsisting between us the undersigned John Andrews Wardell and George Rackshaw as coal and salt merchants carried on at Southend, Leigh, Pitsea, and Plaistow, has this day been resolved by mutual consent.*

George Rackshaw disappeared from business life, leaving John Wardell to carry on as a successful coal merchant and colliery agent. His success enabled him to employ two servants from the fishing village. Emma Going and Jane Plumb.

© *Barry Edwards*

Station Masters

All railway stations need a Station Master (they did in the days of steam) and Leigh was no exception, Richard Twist b1827 took on that position soon after it opened. With his wife Mary, and daughter Monimia born 1858 (their son Oliver died at birth in 1856) Richard Twist remained at his post until his death in 1870. Walter Brown was 27 years old and living on Leigh Hill, around the time of the previous station masters demise. So was well placed to step up into the role, one he would hold for twenty years. Walter's railway career began in Witham, his home town, where he was employed as a railway clerk. Marriage and a family came during his time at Leigh Station to Emma Bordell, daughter of a farmer. When he retired from the railway, he became an insurance clerk. His final years were spent on Carlton Terrace, Leigh Hill, where he died in 1912. His replacement at the station was Edward Frederick Dennis b1857 in Kent. Like Walter his career with the railway began in more humble circumstances as a ticket collector at West Ham in 1880. He rose to the rank of Station Master at West Hordon within ten years. His next placement was at Leigh, where his son Allan was born in1894, followed in 1900 by his daughter Margaret.. The family left in 1910 for Upton Park Station. This was around the time that the new station at the bottom of Leigh Hill was opened for business. The first station master here would be Christopher Morris born 1871 Purfleet. He grew up at The Garrison there, which had civil and military families resident. By the time he was twenty, Christopher was in lodgings and employed as a railway porter at Grays, Essex. Within the next ten years he married and worked his way up to station master his first appointment being at Standford-le-Hope. In 1901, he was in charge at Purfleet, before moving to Leigh-on-Sea until 1923. During his time at Leigh, Christoper Morris lived with his family at number 6 The Gardens off Leigh Hill.

George Alfred Chapman, a Londoner, took over from Christopher Morris. Born in Deptford London in 1870. His first position as Station Master was at Hornchurch from 1905 to the 1920s. For a few years after this date he was at Leigh-on-Sea. The final station master in the old town before the new station opened at the bottom of Belton Hills came Ernest Alfred Rouse. A local man, born at Shoeburyness his first placement was in Thurrock as a booking clerk, before promotion to station master at East Tilbury. Arriving at the old station in 1932, he then moved onto the new station at the bottom of Belton Hills.

The down line station 1920s, entrance on New Road
Courtesy of Leigh Sailing Club

Booking Clerks

Late 1800s Ernest Maxted from New Cross in London, worked at Leigh Station, by 1911 he had left to become a ladies tailor. Taking up residence in Balmoral Road Westcliff. The 1900s saw booking clerks coming and going, some like Frederick Seaton Broadbent, whose father James was chief railway clerk at a main line station in London, served for over twenty years. Frederick lived at number 34 Queens Road, Leigh. Percy Charles Davies and Percival Stevens were among those who did not see the railway as long term employers and soon moved on to other occupations. Herbert Allingham born in Kidderminster in 1871, began his railway career at Hendon where he served for two decades. He completed his service at Leigh-on-Sea, where he was a booking clerk from 1910. He died here in 1933. Around the same time Percy Charles Davies from Stoke Newington was a railway clerk.

Railway Porters

Always expected to be smartly turned out, porters were there to assist passengers with their luggage when both boarding or alighting from the train. Some of the porters worked at the original station, in the High Street, others at the new building sited at the bottom of Leigh Hill.

Frederick Cotgrove   b 1846 Leigh-on-Sea
Richard Dye   b 1826 Kent

George Chandler
© *Rory Gibbson*

A Well Deserved Service Watch and Chain
George Chandler 1860—1934

The son of a Rochford agricultural labourer (where George was born) he followed his father to work on the land. Change came in the 1880s when he joined the railway and was employed as a signalman. This was quite a social jump as the railway was considered to offer good employment. George also married in the 1800s to Fanny Elizabeth Law, whose father was a baker on Hadleigh High Street. Their first daughter was born in 1886 when George was working at West Tilbury Station. Another daughter followed two years later. His wife returned to Hadleigh for the birth of their son

Henry in 1890, but when their third daughter came along the couple were living in Pitsea. During this period George changed from signalman to a foreman Porter and in 1899 with the arrival of son Reginald they were living at Leigh-on-Sea. Two more children would be born here in the following four years. In 1901 George and Fanny were living in Leighville Grove, with their six children and three lodgers! John Sanders and Joseph Shelley were both railway porters and Samuel Askew was a carman. The Chandler's would later move to New Road opposite the railway. *It was reported on Friday the 17th August 1928, George Chandler ticket collector at Leigh-on-Sea is retiring after forty seven years service. He had served thirty one years at Leigh Station.*

Herbert Bingley b 1911

Herbert Bingley married local girl Agnes Frost in 1932, they were to have four children, one of whom Marie now lives in the north. Leaving the railway to earn more money for his growing family Herbert became a local milkman. Unfortunately he was to die a few years later, leaving his wife to raise their children alone.

Leonard Charles Deeks from Tilbury and Ernest Bolden from Southend-on-Sea were both lodging at Eaton Villas, New Road with George Chandler and his family. George was a local man born in Rochford, and was a foreman porter.

Herbert Bingley (right) on the old station at Leigh-on-Sea

Midland Railway

On the 8th June 1912, Arthur Lewis Stride chairman and managing director of the London, Tilbury and Southend railway informed staff by a circular, that the Midland Railway Company had brought out the LTS. He thanked them for past service and reassured them that they all had a future with the new company.

Arthur Lewis Stride was a civil engineer and one of the founder members of the LTS

Railway Inspector

In 1911 William Frederick Gorse b 1842 in Lancashire was living on Fairleigh Drive, Leigh with his married daughter and husband who was employed by the railway as a Police Inspector. His career had begun at West Ham in 1881 as a Constable, promotion to sergeant came a few years later and by 1901 he was an Inspector. He died here in Essex in 1924.

Death by the Railway Track

The following tale was sent to me by Michael Hansford, who found a note written by his mother Dorothy Leswell nee Cary who was born at 3 Billett Lane in 1890. With strong connections to the area, her grandfather Carey worked on the sand barges and her uncle Bill on the fishing boats. The note left by Dorothy mentioned her family and their lives in Leigh but in particular an event that her mother Florence Carey (who married Victor Leswell) had witnessed with a young friend whilst crossing the railway footbridge

"My mother wrote, there was an old lady who used to collect chickweed by the railway line, to feed her birds. One day my Mum and her friend were on the bridge as a train was coming. They called to the lady but as she was very deaf she did not hear them. The train came and dragged her body to the station, leaving her head on the line where she had been collecting her chickweed".

29th March 1882

An inquest on the body of Saul Bundock, a boy aged six, who was killed on the 29th March, was held on Easter Monday at the Bell Inn before Mr W Codd Coroner. The jury after seeing the body, went to visit the spot where the accident happened, Mr T A Bundock brother of the deceased and a shipwright identified the body. The deceased was the son of John Bundock, Builder.

1910 built eight compartment bogie 3rd class carriage no 283, as restored by British Rail 1956
Published by kind permission of National Express C2C

Henry Newman of Tilbury, Engine driver said "On Wednesday the 29th March I was the driver of the 2.25 from Southend to Fenchurch Street. I did not see a child as I was oiling the valves just as we approached Leigh. I heard a thud against the side and saw the little boy laying on his back by the nearside of the engine, close to the Coastguards Station. On pulling into Leigh Station we informed the station master that we had knocked a child down". The jury returned a verdict of accidental death.

20th July 1906
The death occurred in Victoria Hospital, Southend of Reginald Murray aged 16 of 70 Chinchilla Road, Southchurch, a goods clerk at Leigh Station. During the afternoon he was talking with a fellow clerk named Herbert Clarke, from the goods side of the platform and accidently stepped back between some trucks which were being shunted and between which he was squeezed sustaining such terrible injuries that he died as stated.

4th February 1921
On the above date the body of a man aged 35 with both legs broken and other injuries, having been apparently knocked down and run over by a train was discovered by the track. In the man's pocket were papers bearing the name Gibbs. Subsequently the body was identified as that of Rollinson Charles Gibbs.

8th June 1929
Mr Hugh Llewellyn aged 56 of Leigh collapsed and died while playing bridge on a train travelling from Southend to Fenchurch Street. Inquest showed he had died due to a cerebral haemorrhage.

Fire at the Railway Station 27th May 1895

Leigh Fire Brigade
D Hope©
his Uncle James Clarke was a Leigh-on-Sea fireman

At a quarter past four in the morning the night watchman at Browns Mill discovered the railway station on fire (not the one at the bottom of Leigh Hill). Having summoned the fire brigade they arrived shortly just before five o'clock. By this time the station, which was a wooden structure and has been frequently complained about as being totally inadequate for the requirements of Leigh-on-Sea, was burning fiercely. Within the hour the flames were subdued. The damage was estimated at £200.

Railway Officials 14th March 1897

A visit from Railway officials on Thursday, on a special saloon carriage, journeyed from Fenchurch Street to Leigh conveying a deputation representing the officials of the London Tilbury and Southend Railway. A survey was made properly to consider the sight of a new railway station (this was constructed and today is the home of Leigh Sailing Club).

All that is left today (2013) of the old station platform

8th October 1897

As the Sunday afternoon local train from Southend-on-Sea was being shunted onto the down line at the station it failed to properly clear the points, with result that one of the carriages and a portion of the platform were damaged. No one was hurt.

The interior of Leigh Sailing Club. This area used to be the booking office for the railway station.

New Railway Bridge—Wednesday 31st October 1876

The day on which the new railway bridge was opened, there were some children clattering down the steps of the bridge, making so much noise that they frightened a horse. The poor creature bolted and broke down the fence of Mr Fosters garden at Pittington House on New Road.

In 1881 on the self same bridge during the evening of October 14th 1881, a Mrs Thompson of New Road was crossing over, to take some cakes to the bake house. As well as carrying the cakes she also had a baby in her arms. At the foot of the bridge her foot was caught and she fell down and fractured two of her ribs. She was attended by Mr Phillips, surgeon. The baby escaped with a few bruises.

Letter to the Editor of the Chelmsford Chronicle—6th September 1878

Sir
This busy station has improved in various ways of late, but a sad necessity is felt in the want of longer platforms on both sides of the line, traffic having so much increased. This must cause great anxiety to the guards and porters as well as the respected Station Master. The public feel the inconvenience according to their age , habits and sex while all alike run considerable risks in frequently having to jump from the carriage to the ground, a distance of some feet. The dark evenings are coming and it is unfair on the inhabitants and visitors, should be left liable to such dangers that are very likely to occur.

Capture of a Pocket Fish—20th February 1880

A Pocket Fish three feet in length was on Thursday caught by Mr J Gilson, in the Creek at the commencement of the flood tide. The fish had taken refuge in a hole during low water and was getting ready to meet the rising tide when it was caught by Mr Gilson. It has an enormous mouth and bit violently the foot of young William Frost, a lad with Mr Gilson. The fish was brought to Leigh Railway Station and placed in a tank kept there as a receptacle for rare fish suitable for the Westminster Aquarium.

Prosperity and Change

The arrival of the railway brought great change and prosperity to Leigh-on-Sea, even though the heart of the village was lost in the name of progress. And the once tranquil area would now have the noise and smoke of giant steam engines thundering through its heritage. For two years the station was the terminus for the LTS before pushing on to Southend and the end of the line at Shoeburyness. With the fisherman's catch now reaching Billingsgate market in half the time it took by road, there was a dramatic increase in the amount of fish of every kind, that was harvested and sent up to the city. Traffic was not just one way, as Londoners wanting a day by the sea, enjoying its fresh clean air and the opportunity to relax, came in their hundreds. Some to stay in boarding houses, others just for the day, providing customers for the cafes and the fish stalls. Further developments came with speculators buying up land around the immediate vicinity, recognizing the potential in building new and more upmarket housing, for those city workers who wanted to live by the sea, but with fast rail links back to the metropolis continuing working up the line.

Steaming through Leigh Station to the right buildings that used to stand on Leigh Hill.

Signalman King

LONDON TILBURY AND SOUTHEND RAILWAY COMPANY.

MANAGER'S OFFICE,
FENCHURCH STREET TERMINUS,
LONDON, E.C., 27th August, 1900.

LD, No. 1/240.

Conditions of Service of Signalmen, Assistant Signalmen and Porter-Signalmen.

The Directors have agreed that from and including the week which ended on the 6th instant, the Conditions of Service (Hours of Duty, Rates of Pay, Allowances, &c.) of Signalmen, Assistant Signalmen and Porter-Signalmen will be as under:—

WEEKLY SCALE OF PAY OF SIGNALMEN.

SIGNALMEN.	1st YEAR.	2nd YEAR.	3rd YEAR.	4th YEAR.
Special Class	28/-	28/-	27/-	28/-
1st "	24/-	25/-	25/-	26/-
2nd "	23/-	24/-	25/-	26/-
3rd "	22/-	23/-	24/-	25/-
5th "	20/-	21/-	22/-	23/-

Signalmen in Special and 1st Class Cabins who have held that position for 6 years will be paid 1/-; and who have been employed in Special or 1st Class Cabins 10 years will be paid 2/- per week in excess of this scale.
Signalmen in 2nd Class Cabins who have held that position for 6 years will be paid 1/- per week in excess of this scale.
These advances, as is the case with all others, are contingent upon the men concerned having a good record.
An allowance of 3/- per week will be allowed to all Signalmen in the London District up to and including Barking East Junction Signal-box in all cases where the Company does not provide Cottages at a rent not exceeding 1/- per week, and this allowance will be made until the Company is prepared to offer the Signalmen cottages at a rent not exceeding 1/- per week.

CLASSIFICATION OF BOXES AND HOURS OF DUTY.

FIRST CLASS.	Daily Hours of Duty	SECOND CLASS.	Daily Hours of Duty	THIRD CLASS.	Daily Hours of Duty	FOURTH CLASS.	Daily Hours of Duty	FIFTH CLASS.
Upton Park	8	Little Ilford No. 3	8	Upminster East Jnc.	10	Upney	10	Romford
East Ham No. 1	8	East Ham Loop Jnc.	10	West Thurrock Jnc	10	Dagenham	10	East Horndon
Little Ilford No. 1	8	Woodgrange Park Jc	10	Grays East	10	Hornchurch	10	Laindon
Little Ilford No. 2	8	Upminster	10	Tilbury North Jnc.	10	Rippleside	10	Ockendon
Barking East	8	Grays West	10	Tilbury Docks	10	Dagenham Dock	10	West
		Tilbury West Junc.	10	Tilbury East Junc.	10	Rainham	10	Low Street
		Tilbury South Junc	10	Pitsea Junction	10	Ordnance Crossing	10	Thorpe
		Southend	10			Purfleet	10	Stanford
		Shoeburyness	10			Bonfleet	10	
						Leigh	10	
						Westcliff	10	

Assistant Signalmen in the London District and at Tilbury South Junction to be classed as fourth-rate Signalmen.

Goods Yard today used as storage by Leigh Sailing Club

The Goods Yard viewed from Bell Wharf

The railway line today.

The footbridge from New Road which takes you into the Old Town is currently closed.
(2013)

Today passengers travel from the station opened in 1932. Leigh Station stands at the bottom of Belton Hills.

Protecting the Coast
Custom Officers and Coastguards

Smuggling was a way of life for the inhabitants of Leigh-on-Sea, throughout the 17th and 18th

Century. Not that Essex was alone in this pursuit of evading duty on goods, as most of England's coastline paid witness to the illegal contraband being brought into the country. Goods such as tea, coffee, wine, brandy and gin as well as silk and lace came ashore under the cover of darkness. It was estimated during the 18th century, that between fifty and sixty five percent of spirits consumed during this period, were smuggled goods. The penalty for these activities, depended on a number of factors, the value of the goods smuggled and if violence was used against the Coastguard or Custom Officers. The ultimate sentence therefore would be death.

Coastguard Station

Essex Record Office provided the first available records of a Custom Officer at Leigh which occurred between 1732–1736. William Foster was the Collector during this period and complained.

"The Custom House is not convenient for business there being no room for no person but themselves. There being another room at the house where he is fixt that stands facing the river

but there is no place for a fire. The rent of this house is six pounds per ann."

It appears that the building was leased for some twenty one years. In 1808 it was purchased by The Crown for the sum of £350 and the present building still standing on the High Street today, was erected by Thomas Hill in 1815. Costs recorded in an annual account as follows:

Barry Edwards ©

April 1817 building and repairs to contract at Leigh	£291
22nd April balance for building the Custom House	25.3.8d
For erecting the Privy	12.– .–
Second instalment for building the warehouse	97..– .–

The full cost of erecting the new Custom House was £450, including using the old materials from the former building. The beam over the archway today is clearly re-used timber, the slots along its edge probably supported floor joists.

In 1856 the London, Tilbury and Southend Railway put in a bid for the property and it is thought an offer was also made with regard to the Watch House or Coastguard Station. The records state that a new combined building was provided, but does not make clear when or where this combined building stood. The Custom service carried on in the town using their original building until 1881, when it was withdrawn, as trade at the port had diminished. However Custom Officers lodged close by (Coastguard Cottages in the Gardens off Leigh Hill) to continue their fight against smuggling, into the 1900s. The coastguard building remained for another twenty years before being demolished to make way for railway sidings for the new station at the bottom of Leigh Hill.

For those serving at Leigh-on-Sea from the 17th century onwards, one rule that affected them all was, that they were not to be local people or marry into the families of Old Leigh. This was to prevent collusion. However in the very early years there were two men who were born and bred here. One of whom was William Henry King, born in 1788. When he died in 1858 he was buried in St Clements churchyard. William King was the Collector of Taxes. The other was Joseph Ingram 1772–1852, Custom Officer, born at Leigh-on-Sea as was his wife. Like William King he retired here, living on Leigh Hill until the end of his days. Thereafter my research has shown that Coastguards and Custom Officers came from all parts of England, Scotland and Ireland to serve for a few months or several decades in Old Leigh. I have listed a few of the men whose time was spent here trying to prevent smuggling and collecting taxes, from the 1850s until the early 1900s.

1850s–1890s
William H May—Coastguard b.1828 Folkstone, Kent. Daughter Harriett born at Leigh 1850, followed by two more children. The family moved to the coastguard station at Great Wakering by 1860.

Joseph Collier—Coastguard b 1822 Portsmouth. Served a short time at Leigh where daughter Mary was born in 1852 , before moving two years later to Burnham.

Edward Green—Coastguard b. 1807 Sussex. Came to Leigh around 1846 and served here for over twenty years. He lived out his retirement where he had served as a Coastguard until his death in 1888.

William Tozer—b1814 Devon. Chief Coastguard/Boatman. Came to Leigh in 1855 and served the coastguard until 1871. Took up residence on the High Street, living on his pension until he died in 1888.

Joseph Collier b 1822 Portsmouth—Coastguard. First posting was at Burnham then on to Leigh -on-Sea where he served from 1850–1854.

Thomas Gowland b 1806 Canterbury, Kent—Coastguard. Postings to Ireland, Cornwall and Hadleigh in Essex, came before his time in Leigh between 1849–1860, when with his family he was posted to Greenwich, Kent.

Thomas George b 1828 Tiverton, Devon
William Pascal b 1827 Cornwall—Coastguards in 1860s.

Charles Wallace b1830 Sussex—Boatman/Coastguard. Charles served at Leigh-on-Sea from 1865–1891. During this period his son Walter took a job with the local railway, having employment first as a Porter/Clerk. Promotion followed a few years later and he was to be found as the Station Master at Upminster. When retirement came for Charles Wallace he moved to Burnham, Essex.

David Verner b 1841 Ireland—Coastguard Royal Navy. He came to Leigh-on-Sea in 1871 with his wife Penelope who unfortunately died the following year. David Verner was to follow his wife a few years later in 1878 whilst still living at Leigh-on-Sea.

William Cummings b1836 Portsmouth—Chief Collector of Taxes. Time spent at Leigh was from 1879–1890, when he moved on to East Ham.

Edward Sicely b 1837 Devon—Boatman, Leigh-on-Sea 1870s
Thomas Nichols b 1841 Cornwall—Coastguard.
James Fox b 1849 Bristol Coastguard Leigh-on-Sea 1883–1890

Connections

When George Terry b 1826, Suffolk—Coastguard was posted to Maldon in Essex, he served with Edward Sicely—boatman. Because of this he met and married one of his sisters Catherine Mary Sicely in 1846. Later both men would find themselves at Leigh-on-Sea. but not during the same period, Edward Sicely was in the 1870s, when George Terry and wife Catherine with their last child, Flora, were stationed at Shoeburyness, where their daughter was born in 1867. Although the Terry's would do another term of service back in Maldon they returned to this area in the late 1890s, where they took up residence at Leigh-on-Sea, where until his death in 1906 George and his wife remained.

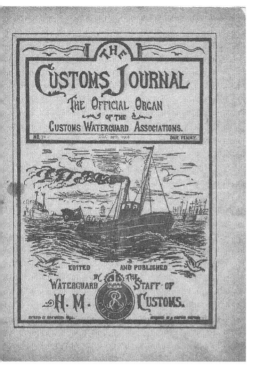

Thomas Stokes b.1838 Buckinghamshire—Coastguard from 1879–1882
George Graham b.1828 Deal, Kent—Chief Boatman/Coastguard 1881–1883
Frederick Hext b. 1840 Devon—Coastguard 1878–1885.

1900s

Joseph Walton b.1869 Birmingham—Coastguard Boatman.
William Higgins b.1861 Bristol—Coastguard here from 1894–1901
Henry Bryant b.1864 London—Coastguard .
Sidney C Hodges b.1870 Somerset—Coastguard. Living in the coastguard cottages, The Gardens, Leigh Hill.
Charles T Symonds b 1869 Cornwall—Coastguard here early 1900s. By 1911 Charles was a petty officer and serving in Yorkshire.
Henry James Dimery b.1861 Gloucester Coast at Leigh from 1890–1900.

William Brinkley b.1849 Kent—Station Navy Officer. He was stationed at Leigh from 1894–1901. After this date I have been unable to locate his next posting. His father Thomas also served in the Coastguard. Accommodation during William Brinkley's time here was No 1 Mardy Villas, West Street, Leigh-on-Sea. During the 1880s he served as a boatman on H.M.S Penelope. Retirement when it came around 1905, saw William Brinkley moving back to Kent.

Arthur Margrave b 1857 Herfordshire—Chief Custom Officer. Served on H.M.S Druid, in the 1880s. He only served two years at Leigh between 1908–1910. He died the following year having transferred to Whitechapel in London.

John Bryan b.1859 Norfolk—Chief Coastguard from 1910–1914 lived in one of the coastguard cottages in The Gardens, Leigh Hill. He remained in the area after retirement, until he passed away in 1959 in Southend-on-Sea..

Alexander Atrill b.1870 Isle Of Wight Chief Petty Officer/Coastguard. 1906–1911
Thomas Offer b.1872 Clapham—Coastguard 1906–1911.

Charles John Huxstep

© *Charles Huxstep*

I was fortunate to be contacted by a Charles Huxstep, living locally, with regard to his grandfather Charles John Huxstep. Because of this contact I am able to give an a more in-depth account into his ancestors time in the Royal Navy and then as a coastguard. between 1882 -1891 at Leigh on sea. I was also provided with the photographs that appear with this piece, showing the man himself and his family who would have moved around the country with him.

Charles Huxstep 1855–1932—Coastguard

Charles story is one of hard work that began when he was born in Kent in 1855, suffering from bow legs. His father determined that his son should be able to walk normally, carried him down each morning to the sea, where he gathered seaweed. Boiling water in an old tin bath he added the seaweed, which was then wrapped around his son's legs. This continued for a number of weeks until at last his son's legs were straightened. Because of his father's determination to give his son a normal life, Charles went on to have a career in the Royal Navy and the Coast Guard.

His working life began as labourer in Wingfield, Kent where he lived with his family. By the time he was 21 and married with one child, he was serving in the Royal Navy (coxswain) having signed up for 12 years. His papers describe him as , 5ft 6inches tall, with a fair complexion, light brown hair and blue eyes. During his naval career Charles Huxstep served on The Duke of Wellington, The Excellent, Boadica and The Royal Adelaide.

Leaving the Navy around 1882 Charles went straight into the service of the coastguards (this was quite a common occurrence for sailors leaving the navy). Posted to Leigh on sea his daughter Lousia (b1888) and son Joseph(b1890) were born during this posting to Essex. Moving back to the Kent area in 1891, he served for another ten years before retiring, the 1911 census shows him living on his navy pension and working as a caretaker for a council school. A hard working man all his life, this was reflected in a reference written for him in 1903, which described him as "an honest and sober man, intelligent and active".

© C Huxstep

When one of sons (another Charles) moved to Essex, Charles senior came to visit him and his family in 1932. Here he died peacefully in his sleep.

The Gas Works

THE GAS QUESTION—A large and important meeting was held in the Sailors' Rest on Tuesday night to consider the question of adopting gas or otherwise. Hitherto the fishermen have foiled any attempt to light the town with gas at the expense of the parish, and as a result two years ago the principal tradesmen put up 10 lamps and have since maintained them by voluntary subscriptions. The parish was now asked to take the matter in hand. The Rev. Canon King presided. The room was crowded. Mr Smith said that during the last six months the Gas Works had been carried on at a considerable loss, and unless public lighting with gas were adopted there was but one alternative, viz, to close them. It was proposed to enter into an agreement to light the streets for three years, and to levy a small rate of 4d. In the pound per annum, which on cottage property would only mean 1s. 4d or 1s 8d a year. The proceedings were most disorderly. After a long discussion a decision was taken, when it was found that 83 were in favour of the gas and 27 against. The meeting broke up in great confusion.

The first gas lighting outside of London, was in Preston Lancashire in 1825. And was a company run by the Rev. Joseph Dunn. With gas lighting up to 75% cheaper than using candles or oil lamps, it comes as no surprise that this helped to accelerate its development, as a reliable and cost effective way to light the streets and people's homes. Gas lighting paved the way for English factories to work longer hours through the winter months. The majority of gas works were built by rivers or canals and later they would stand near a railway line, all three options allowed the easy delivery of coal.

The Leigh Gas and Light company was formed in 1866 and the gas works were first in operation in Leigh around 1873 (in 1899 the council brought out the local gas works under their private act of that year) although it was clear that not all the residents of the town were keen to have this new form light and heat, in their homes. Today, come over and down the flyover into the High Street , you will be greeted by the Osborne's fish establishment. The gas works used to stand in the area behind Osborne's.

Leigh Gas Works

Searching through old newspapers I found the following reports connected to the Gas works:

On Saturday 20th May 1871 a horse belonging to Mr D. Tomlin, being loose, strayed onto the unfinished gas works and began drinking from a tank, filled with water. Unfortunately he stepped forward and became fully immersed being unable to extradite himself. The scene which followed and the work getting him out caused some excitement, but luckily the animal was less hurt than frightened.

The New Road

February 1883. The railway company has during the past week, agreed to the request of the gas company and given permission for gas pipes to be laid along New Road. Which at a meeting in the vestry the parishioners refused to take over as a Parish Road

Accident

May 1883 A large cylinder for use at the gas works, being carried from the railway station last Monday, the truck being used, broke down. The cylinder weighed about 35cwt and would have caused a considerable obstruction on the narrow High Street, was removed by leverage to the open space by the Strand pump.

Pipe Laying

June 1883. The manager has been very busy during the past week laying pipes for the LTS railway station and a number of private houses also had gas fitted. And we understand work will be finished in the town soon, when the area will be promptly lighted.

An Incident at the Gas Works

November 1883. Monday afternoon the sons of Mr R. Filby were using a crowbar on the gasworks premises, when the younger of the two was struck, the crowbar going completely through his right hand. His father managed to stop the bleeding and took him off to Mr Phillips surgery.

Startling Explosion

23rd December. On Monday morning a gas explosion took place at Leigh-on-Sea, in a manhole in the street, near R F Emery and sons premises. There was a dreadful loud report and the socket of the manhole which was cemented down, was thrown up into the air about 50 feet and fell through the roof of the Blacksmiths shop. Which was tenanted by a Mr Joscelyne. No one was at work at the time. Several people were struck by flying fragments, stones, etc and a number of windows were broken. Sometime later there was a second explosion at the same spot, accompanied by flames and a man was knocked over.

The accident was caused by negligence on the part of the foreman of the gas works, who was later dismissed.

Sale of Gas Works

23rd October 1888. Messers Edwin Fox and Bousfield offered for sale by auction the Leigh gas works. The sale comprised of the building, retort house (contained retorts in which coal was heated to generate gas) and coal store combined, a purifier shed and station meter and governor house. The whole of the plant fittings, sundries, stores etc, included in the sale. The gas works have good frontage of the river Thames. Current owner Edwin Fox.

The property was offered at £400, the price was carried up to £720 at which figure it was knocked down to Messers Parkinson and Co, engineers.

Sudden Death

Henry Howard of North Avenue died suddenly while working at the gas works in September 1908.

Grand Opening

10th December 1910. The extension of the gas works was opened by Mr Meacben, chairmen of the committee. The new gas holder which cost £1490 has a capacity of 160,000 cubic feet.

Incendiary's 1915

28 incendiary and high explosive bombs dropped by the enemy on Leigh on sea gas works, were later recovered from the foreshore, all having failed to explode.

Death of a Newsagent's Wife, 21st December

Mrs Ellen Thorpe (59) of Leigh Hill died last from gas poisoning. On Sunday the lady and her husband—William Thorpe, a newsagent were found unconscious in bed. Mr Thorpe recovered. It is thought the flame on the gas fire accidently went out. Mrs Thorpe had suffered paralysis for two years prior to her death.

A Clergyman's Demise, March 1931

The Rev. Thomas James Longhurst (72) a retired Baptist minister and his wife, were found gassed in their apartment at a house on Pall Mall. A faulty gas tap cased death by gas poisoning.

Manager Owners and Staff

Information available on the various owners of the gas works, their managers and staff, was extremely sparse. What information I could find came mainly from using the census and other local resources. Fortunately two people came forward with photographs of their relatives time at the gas works.

Owners

1888	Fox and Bousfield/ Parkinson and co.
1890/91	George Swinbourne
1899	Samuel White

Managers:

William Whittock from Devizes in Wiltshire worked for the gas company during the late 1890s and was living on the High Street with his wife Elizabeth and unmarried daughter Esther. His whole working life had been in this new industry, starting in 1861 as a stoker. By 1880 he was the foreman of a gas works in Kent before promotion brought him to Leigh-on-Sea and the position of manager. Whilst still working for the gas company at the age of 70 , William died at Leigh-on-Sea in1891.

Moses Bradford
©R Becks

A local man born in Great Wakering in 1857 Moses Edwin Bradford, was the son of a waterman. Edwin as he was known, was a general labourer when first he started work, he continued in this occupation for many years. Living and working in the Prittlewell area with his wife Georgina Osborne and children. Quite how or when he began working for the gas company is unknown, but he was employed as the Manager by 1891 and was still in charge there in 1911. During later years he lived at number 26 Canonsleigh Drive, Leigh with his son Edwin—a gas fitter, living at

Moses Bradford and Wife
©R Becks

number 20 with his family. Lodging with Edwin, was one Arthur Ludwig of German decent, who was a gas fitters plumber. Another of Moses' sons, Percy, worked for the company, collecting rent, due on gas stoves and other appliances.

Throughout the 1920s a Thomas Frederick Canning was the engineer and manager, at Leigh (he later moved to Southend) as the company was now known as the Southend and District Gas Company. By 1933 he was living in Thorpe bay.

General Hands and Labourers

During the 1900s workers came and went, William Wakerling b1862 Hadleigh Essex, living on the High Street at no 48, in the early 1900s, occupation gasman. Within a few years he was lodging with a Mary Plumb (widow) from 1911 at number 5 Theobald Cottage. Also sharing the house was Walter Houghton, another gasman. Walter was Leigh born and bred (1865) the son of a fisherman. Before becoming a gasman, Walter had been a general labourer, living with his parents and siblings on the High Street. First on The Strand, later Alley Dock. He never married. At number 3 Theobald Cottages during the same decade, lived Walter Bowers from Oxford (b1872) his occupation given as stoker at council gas works. Ten years previously he was working as a baker and confectioner. Quite a change of occupation. From around 1911 John Carter, Walter Bowers and Henry Thomas Dunn were all employed as gas stokers. Walter lodged at number 3 Theobalds Cottage, while Henry and John lived on Church Hill. Local man William Turnidge and Charles Daries, from Buckinghamshire, both worked for several years as labourers for the gas company.

Further details of those employed by the gas company in later years have not been forthcoming. But a meeting with Carol Cass granddaughter of John Henry Meddle has enabled me to show a photograph of some of the employees in the 1920s. John Meddle 2nd from left

John Henry Meddle

John Meddle son of Stephen a fisherman was born Leigh-on-Sea in 1875. He lived with his family for over twenty years at Cottage Place, New

John Meddle, back row, standing second from the lef
C Cass ©

Road. John took various occupations throughout his life, including coal sweeping at the gas works around 1911. John Meddle married Charlotte Osborn in 1898 and they lived, as did many Meddle's at Townfield Place (the area is now a road leading to the flyover).

During 1953 the Borough Engineer reported that the condition of the old gas works building on the east side of the High Street, was now in such a state as to render it dangerous to the public, he recommended that steps be taken immediately for it's demolition at the estimated cost of eighty pounds.

The area today (2013) where once the gas works stood is now a pleasant promenade and café

© *Barry Edwards*

Hubert Clarkson born in London the son of a member of the Stock Exchange. He came to Essex around 1900 where he married his wife Emily, his daughter Doris was born here in 1903. Hubert Clarkson returned to London in the 1930s.

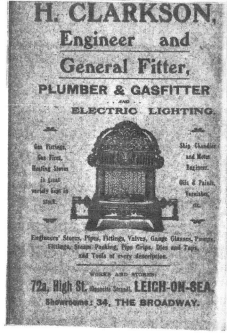

Advert 1913

The building of the Retort House.

The Gas works was divided into several sections for the production and purification and storage of gas. The retort house contained the "retorts" in which were coal was heated to generate the gas . The waste product left in the retort was coke.

D/BC 1/4/10/11/146
Leigh Gas Works, 30 March, 1915

Photographs by kind permission of Essex Record Office

D/BC 1/4/10/11/145
Leigh Gas Works 30 March 1915

Supplying The Town With Coal

Leigh Heritage Centre

Coal was an important commodity to Leigh as it was to the rest of the country following the industrial revolution. Used by the local gas works to provide heat and light for street lamps and the railway to power their engines. With coal in abundance as opposed to wood, it was also sold to householders to light their fires and fuel their ovens to cook their meals. The coal yard also offered employment, from sweeping the yard, bagging the coal for sale or in Victor Leswell's case, to drive coal filled horse drawn carriages to Hadleigh and elsewhere in the local district. Victor married Florence Carey in 1918 and for a time they lived on Billet Lane, where his wife had been born at number three (in 1920 their daughter Dorothy would be born here—her son Mike Hansford still lives locally). During the 1840s James Lucking was lodging at the Kings Head, owned at that time by William Foster, who was also a coal merchant. It is quite probable therefore, that James worked for his landlord. In the 1870s Alfred West was a foreman coal porter, having first tried his hand as a baker. His father Daniel was the Blacksmith on Leigh Hill. A small number of coal dealers on the High Street, only dabbled in the commodity for a short period, others were there for decades. With all this coal being burnt in the Old Town the services of a Chimney Sweep were required and in 1906 Arthur Martin a young man in his twenties was living at number 22 the High Street. He offered his services to the residents to keep their chimneys clean.

Coal Merchants

William Foster, advertised his coal in an Essex newspaper
> W.F. begs to inform the public his present price for coals is—good Seconds
> 16/s Best 18/s a ton at the Kings Wharf Leigh, for ready money
> 8th June 1849

In April 1859 at Rochford Petty Sessions, William Finch a labourer was brought under remand and charged with stealing a quantity of coal from William Foster. He was committed for six weeks. In that same month Foster himself was summoned by Inspector Ackers for having unjust weights and fined 5s with costs of 9d.

As you will read in the section devoted to the Kings Head Public House, where William Foster was for a time the landlord, you will discover that far from just selling coal, he was a man of many interests.

Coal Order Office: THE BROADWAY.

T. TOMLIN & SONS,

Coal and Coke Merchants,

IRONMONGERS, CARMEN, and CONTRACTORS,

ROPE, YARN and SAIL CLOTH, Manufacturers.

Victoria Wharf, Leigh-on-Sea, Essex

The Tomlin family including Michael, who went on to become a well know preacher and Daniel who in the 1900s was the Sanitary Inspector of Leigh Urban Town Council, the family had all been fishermen. They were the sons of David Tomlin and Mary Frost. Thomas and Oswald went into the coal trade but with Oswald's death in 1901 this just left Thomas Tomlin to carry on alone into the 1930s. By the 1800s the Tomlin brothers were established on the High Street selling more than just coal. In later years, quite remarkable for the time Thomas's daughter Lydia was listed in 1911 as living at number 4 High Street, occupation Boot Repairer/Coal Merchant!

From fisherman to coal merchant, Edgar Kirby born in the old town in 1868, was a coal dealer on the High Street, from the late 1880s and was still listed as a coal merchant when he was 74 years old. He was also in business with his brother Frederick on the High Street as Ship Chandlers. Edgar and his family lived first in the Old Town, then on New Road before moving to Lymington Avenue, Leigh. Edgar's wife Sarah was the daughter of George Bradley who in the 1880s was the Blacksmith on Joscelyne Square. The Kirby coal business would be carried on by Edgar Kirby's son—another Edgar (b1899) into the 1940s.

Thomas Tomlin continued to sell coal until the 1930s. William Partridge offered coal for sale from number 65 High Street from 1880–1911.

William Lungley (1811-1889) in 1850 his son William was working as a Coal Porter. This may have inspired William Snr to become a Coal Merchant during the 1860s. By 1870 he was working as a Carman. Frederick Bayford was also a Coal Dealer for a few years

In December 1952 until March 1953, a deadly smog covered London. This was due to a period of really cold weather, coupled with an anti cyclone and windless conditions. So when Londoners burnt more coal than usual to keep warm (fuel after the Second World War was low grade) the smog simply covered the Capital with no way of dispersing this deadly smoke. Thousands would die because of poor air quality. In 1956 the clean air act was implemented, when smokeless fuels were encouraged and the use of gas and electricity as forms of heating and cooking became more readily used.

The Forge

The Forge
By permission of Leigh Heritage Centre

In every small town or village from the middle ages, there would have been a blacksmith at the heart of the community, playing a vital role in the daily lives of the population. At Leigh-on-Sea there were at different times two maybe three blacksmiths, sharing the forge on the High Street. Another was to be found on Leigh Hill. The blacksmith would burn coal or charcoal on his forge, forcing up the heat when needed with the use of bellows. With much of the area around the High Street, farms and small holdings, the majority of the blacksmiths work would have been repairing agricultural equipment. Work would have also come from making anchors and chains to secure the fishing boats and in time of war the blacksmith could be called upon to fashion swords and other weapons. Cooking utensils, and other household items would have made at the forge for the locals basic needs. Today in the Old Smithy, preserved by the Leigh Society can be seen the tools and some of the artefacts made there over the decades.

Blacksmiths

From the 1850s right through until 1895 a "Churchyard" was the blacksmith at Leigh. George Churchyard born in Canewdon, Essex in 1827 was first apprenticed to a wheelwright in Rochford when he was 15 years old. He moved to Leigh, where his occupation was now given as blacksmith, in 1851 he married Dorcus Ritchie, daughter of a Leigh fisherman. The couple had two children Caroline 1853 and Henry George Freeman Churchyard in 1855, who took over from his father following his death in 1888 (his mother Dorcus had died in 1876) Henry was to be at the forge for only seven years before his own demise.

As mentioned previously there was often more than one blacksmith serving the old town during the same period. George James Bradley arrived in Leigh in 1868 took up residence on Joscelyn Square, just before the birth of his daughter Alice. From nearby Southend-on-Sea, where he was born in 1840 his father John was also a blacksmith. Although George and his wife produced three sons, not one followed their father's profession. Ernest became a grocer, with Stanley and Archibald taking up employment with the railway as porters. One daughter Sarah married Edgar Kirby (local coal dealer). George remained as a blacksmith in Leigh until retirement in the early 1900s.

George James Bradley died in 1914.

Around 1881 William Tanner born on the Isle of Wight, was here working as a blacksmith, his stay was short lived.

By kind permission of Leigh Heritage Centre

Past and Present

The old town with its long high street, has continued to evolve over the decades. Today with its unique atmosphere of old combined with new, still attracts visitors from far and wide as well as the local population all year round.

Billet Wharf, in the background The Crooked Billet.

This is the same area today, where Osborne's serve fresh fish and refreshments.

Belton Cottages
By kind permission of Leigh Heritage Centre

These cottages were among the poorest in the old town as these photographs show.

Their long gardens used to stretch up Belton Hills. They would be lost to the railway in the 1850s. All these dwellings have since been demolished.

1950s.

1940s.

The steps to the right of this photograph led to the footbridge over the railway.
Frank Bridge's shop is second from left.

A winters morning in the old town. 1940s

A view taken in the early 1900s

The large building on the left is The Smack Public House.
Opposite used to stand the original railway station

One of the many establishments
that offered refreshments.

This photograph was taken in 1941 in the same area as the picture opposite—to the right was the railway station. The café and surrounding buildings have now been demolished. Previous owners in the 1920s were a Mr and Mrs Cotgrove who sold pales and spades, minerals (drinks), tobacco and cigarettes, confectionary, ice cream, rock, and tea.

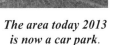

*The area today 2013
is now a car park.*

The level crossing that used to stand at the bottom of Leigh Hill. Opposite is The Ship Public House and to the left of the cyclists waiting to cross, is the old signal box.

This photograph is taken in the 1960s
© R Morse

This building currently on the High Street today, took its name from The Coal Hole, the pub that used to stand next to The Smack Public House. Today it is the home of the 4th/6th Leigh-on-Sea, Scout Group.

Leigh Regatta
Photographs by kind permission Leigh Heritage Centre.

Regatta 1908.

*Presentation of prizes
20th August 1955*

The winning pull of the Tug of War contest between the Leigh Fisherman and Southend Police on Bell Wharf, 20th August 1955.

Having travelled through the history of the people, buildings and events of Old Leigh, what does the area offer today? The fishing industry still has its place, with boats leaving on the tide to catch fish for the home market and beyond. Seafood is still available from the small sheds dotted along the narrow road that runs beside the railway.

This view was taken in the 1920s and shows farm buildings on Belton Hills and in the distance a row of houses now demolished. To the right of the railway line can be seen the cockle sheds still there today. (2013)
© Peter Haddon
(Yesterstreet)

If you enter the town over the wide flyover, you pass the Crooked Billet to your left, Cotgrove's restaurant to the right. Further on a modern frontage is the entrance to the art gallery of Sheila Appleton and the pottery of Richard Baxter (see forward).

Having passed the Peter Boat public house on your right, a cafe occupying space on the small bend in the road is next. A few paces more and you have reached the Lynn Tait Gallery

On the same side of the road stands the Old Custom House (now privately owned) and just across the cobbled road there is another café and the Heritage Centre.

Heritage Centre

With free entry to its museum and restored fisherman's cottage, the walls are lined with photographs and information on those who have lived and worked in Leigh, contributing to its history. Including those who went to Dunkirk on the little ships.

The museum which is open seven days a week, is run by volunteers (hours vary)

One more public house, The Smack, before reaching the shops selling, sweets, ice cream , buckets and spades and all things expected of the seaside. Next door to complete the tradition, fish and chips. At the far end of the High Street you will find the Fisherman's Co-op.

Walk on past this building and you're final destination will be the beach.

Families still live on the High Street today, however, there are far fewer cottages to rent or own due to the mass of demolition carried out in the name of progress. With the area very popular with visitors and locals, to have a home here today, you must be prepared to put up with crowds of people filling the pavement outside your windows during the busy summer months

Sheila Appleton

Today you will still find one of the original members of the art group, with a studio on the High Street, where for the past twenty one years Sheila Appleton has shared the space first with Richard Baxter and now with Richard and his wife Kate. For Sheila who was a student at Southend Art College in the 1940s painting is very much still an integral part of her daily life, even though she is past her 80th birthday! Born in a Westcliff-on-Sea nursing home (where coincidently Richard Baxter would be born many years later) Sheila's first home in Leigh was at Bank House on Leigh Hill, during the 1950s and just down the Hill a shop/gallery she

An early Sheila Appleton, of depicting Leigh High Street

shared with two other ladies. Her first commission for a painting came when she was working at Dixons department store at the top of Southend High Street, when the owner Mr Dixon paid her to paint a picture of her choice. "I think he was a little surprised at my choice" laughed Sheila. Her decision to depict a line of men and women queuing to fill their buckets with coke at the old gas works on the seafront.

Success

The Beecroft Art Gallery have purchased three of her paintings, her erotic fairies had a mention on radio four in an interview with Professor Laurie Taylor. And Sheila has won various awards such as the 1965 Silver Palette chosen by Bernard Dunstan ARA.

Described in one of the Leigh-on-Sea official guides as being a "delicious eccentric" I feel having met Sheila Appleton this is a wonderful description of her.

Sheila in her studio today (2013)
© B Edwards

Richard Baxter

I have known Richard Baxter for many years , first as a fan with my younger daughter of the "Famous Potatoes" who have played many times in Old Leigh. Then as a potter, I have visited and purchased a number of his works, from his studio on the High Street.

The studio used to be part of Southend Marine Engineering Company and during the Second World War the premises was used to make shell cases, mainly by a female workforce. Following the war it returned to its former business. Prior to the engineering company it had been used by Arthur Parsons– Boat Builder.

Richard Baxter working in his studio (2013)
© *Barry Edwards*

The Gallery

The building on the rightwas originally the United Brethren Beer House. Later used by the Southend Engineering Company before conversion into Old Leigh Studios. Photograph taken in 1985

The exterior of the Old Leigh Studios on the High Street today (2013)

A collection of photographs on this page, some taken by Richard Baxter after purchasing the building with Sheila Appleton, show its former usage and general decay, before conversation into the bright modern studio it is today.

How the interior looked before conversion into The Studio.

The man in the photograph is John Chapman who worked for The Southend Engineering Company.

A Waterside Soliloquy
By Archie Kirby

Archie Kirby was born 1900 at Leigh-on-Sea. His father Stephen was a fisherman who lived in the Old Town for many years, before moving to Leighville Grove, where Archie was brought up.

One of my pleasures and interests is to visit the Old Town area of Leigh now and again during the summer and observe the holiday scenes. Yachts racing and sailing, the happy shouts of children as they splash about in the water, holiday makers lazing in deckchairs or sunbathing on the beach. All make up an environment of healthy recreation and enjoyment. Another interesting activity to me, is the boat building. Now as one who has been connected with and sailed boats from an early age, at first solo but later "shipping" a crew "hand" who eventually signed on for life (in a church) I have always been interested in watching vessels being built, especially the sailing kind, seeing them take graceful shape under the skilled hands of the builders, then the launch as the boat sits proud upon the water. An enthusiast could almost be pardoned for imaging that a boat could have a conscious personality of its own that it might be thinking. Come master spread my wings and let us get under way, I am ready to take you wherever you want to steer me. Yes why not ye mortals, don't we function under the same conditions and give faithful service to our owners in all weathers and without complaint. It was whilst ruminating thus that certain lines began to run through my head, then grouped themselves into a semblance of order and rhyme so that upon on reaching home and taking up pen and paper the following verses ensured:

Build me straight o worthy master
Taunt and sound and strong
Trim my sails and set the courses
For the voyage may be long

Build me straight o worthy master
With skilled devoted hands
Come aboard and take the helm
Steer me clear of rocks and sand

Build me straight o worthy master
That I sail the seas of life
Standing by to help my neighbour
Giving aid in need of strife

Thou hast been with us gentle master
And with thy light upon the mast
Guide me back that calm haven
When the voyage of life is past
White wings they never grow weary, they carry me cheerily over the sea